SEEING THE *Forest* THROUGH THE *Trees*

Sylvia Stone

Seeing the Forest Through the Trees
Copyright © 2022 by Sylvia Stone

All rights reserved. No part of this publication may be reproduced, distributed, or transmitted in any form or by any means, including photocopying, recording, or other electronic or mechanical methods, without the prior written permission of the author, except in the case of brief quotations embodied in critical reviews and certain other non-commercial uses permitted by copyright law.

ISBN
978-1-957378-27-5 (Paperback)
978-1-957378-26-8 (eBook)

*THIS BOOK IS DEDICATED TO ALL IN
SEARCH OF INNER PEACE*

ACKNOWLEDGEMENTS:

Thank you to my family for passing down all the right tools with which to strengthen my attributes. You have made this book possible! And a special thanks to friends and extended family for their support throughout my writing process. You have blessed me with encouragement!

TABLE OF CONTENTS

Acknowledgements v

Introduction ix

Chapter 1 1

Chapter 2 9

Chapter 3 21

Chapter 4 31

Chapter 5 47

Chapter 6 65

Chapter 7 77

Chapter 8 101

Chapter 9 117

Chapter 10 129

Chapter 11 143

INTRODUCTION

BELIEVE IT OR NOT, what provokes us to cry makes us stronger. It has been hard for me to understand this as I've spent many years weeping over the unfortunate events in my journey through this life. Holding too tightly to the past without understanding its true value had prevented me from living a joyful life. This concept, this dream of being happy was just that . . . a fleeting dream that I could not make true. I had been stuck in this mindset for so long, asking myself questions like, "Why me? Why can't I be happy? Don't I deserve more? Am I paying some kind of karmic debt? Why have I been forsaken? Why am I here and what's it all for?" These thoughts brought on incredible bursts of self-pity. I sat quietly and asked for guidance, which had become quite a ritual, talking to the air hoping that someone or something was listening and would help. I didn't wish to be a victim anymore of the 'poor me' syndrome that most of us seem to possess. I realized that we are all connected no matter how different we seem to be, through our suffering. We share our stories with each other for various reasons. Sometimes it's to vent. Sometimes it's to project our baggage onto other people. Other times we are just looking for support so that we may be comforted in the hopes of feeling better. I started listening closely to the pains of other people and finally paid attention to the whispers that I have been ignoring all my life. Write. Write it all down and share it! Use it to help someone! For a long time, thoughts like, "But who gives a crap about me and my story? What makes me so interesting that someone would even care to read this?", sabotaged any motivation to follow through. Finally, I decided to rid the fear of the unknown and trust my gut. With that, I thought of the old saying, "You can't see the forest through the trees," which essentially means, "You don't get it! You're not seeing what's right in front of your face!" This became the inspiration for the title of this book. What is life like when you DO see the whole picture?

Every single one of us is so beautifully unique and special. We have tremendous value! I'm hoping that by sharing my story, it will inspire and help others to see and live the awesome life that we are all meant to have regardless of what we were and where we came from. As we look at our true selves, we learn from one another. Most of us are aware of that annoying voice in our heads that never seems to shut up. It conjures all sorts of distorted images and takes us on a daily journey through the realm of non-reality, leaving us feeling all kinds of negative emotions thus ruining our mood, our day, our relationships, our motivation, our life! We are all personally responsible for the depth of our own suffering and don't realize that we have the power to move mountains!

I have been on a path to higher awareness my entire life. There has always been something deep within me that craves mindfulness and elevated truth. I like to think of myself as a student of life hoping for good grades. When I don't pay attention or do my homework, I find myself lost and falling behind, finding it necessary to seek out tutoring to get caught up. Sometimes it comes in the form of a book. Other times it comes in the form of talking with a friend or to God/universe/source/all there is . . . whatever you wish to call it. We have all received a lot of baggage from the conditioning of our parents, people in general, and the environment around us which tends to lead us searching aimlessly for answers. As I look at things now, I see that I have the power to undo all that has been done to me. It's extremely empowering to know that this strange being called 'me' has been formed from all that has passed . . . good and bad. What makes us cry DOES make us stronger. By reflecting on these things in a neutral frame of mind, we undo the damage that others have created for us. We don't need to be sad or angry on a regular basis. We can be rid of fear and anxiety. We can stop blaming others and take responsibility. Ultimately, we can identify our strengths by examining our roots, reclaiming them, and putting all the other crap to bed. Nothing HAS to be difficult anymore!

CHAPTER 1

LITTLE SPROUT

IT WAS THE SUMMER of love in 1969 when Sharon lay alone in a delivery room far from home in Wisconsin. She was well overdue and, when they induced labor, it was long, intense and frightening. The joke was that I didn't want to be born as the nurse cleaned me up and put me in my mother's arms. A mistake? We'd have to see.

A deal was made, and the baby was to be given up for adoption. Leif, the father, refused to accept any responsibility for a child and Sharon's mother, Zofie, was afraid for her nineteen-year-old daughter and voiced that a single mother wouldn't have a chance at a good life. The mindset in those days was very different and full of shame, "What man would want you, already equipped with a kid?" The attempted abortion earlier in the pregnancy hadn't worked. A hot bath had been drawn for Sharon and she was fed dangerous amounts of quinine before being led to a plastic covered mattress that was prepped and ready to receive the aborted fetus. She became violently ill, but something watched over me and I did not die, so it was probably the right decision for her to consider adoption. She was a high school dropout that foolishly chased her first love, Leif, around while she searched for her identity. As he was breaking her heart and she was running from her dysfunctional family, it seemed that all strikes were against her. Taking on a baby would be ludicrous.

The adoption agency walked down the hospital hall and headed to Sharon's room to get her signature and finalize the surrender. As they entered the threshold, they were surprised to find that I was not immediately taken to the nursery, but rather placed in my mother's arms. This was against procedure. "Doesn't the nurse know? The baby should not have been given to her," as they reached for me. Sharon didn't let go and informed the staff that she had changed her mind.

My mother later told me that during the time she held me in that room all alone, I looked at her and she fell in love. She said, "I didn't know what kind of a mother I'd be, but I would try to be the best I could!" She wrote letters to her parents, Loosha and Zofie. She wrote to Leif's parents, Rita and Teddy, informing every one of her decision. She still loved my father and chose to lie to social services, claiming she didn't know who the father was as to absolve him from any responsibility.

What now? Even the doctor who delivered me knew that Sharon had absolutely nothing. The day she brought me home to her shabby little apartment, she was greeted by a room full of flowers and a crib, all sent by her doctor. Mom was pretty much alone and knew it was best she made it back home to Ohio soon. Dad had his own place here in Wisconsin, attending college, and he found a little time to meet me and gave me my name. He wrote a letter to his mother saying, "I'm getting to know her. She's really a happy kid and fun to be around! I'll be coming home soon to visit."

When the time came to leave Wisconsin, the angels watched over me again when a last-minute change of plans postponed my leaving with Dad and his sister in his van. For some reason, my mother and I stayed behind for a few days while the van took a roll and tumble on the highway. I would have surely perished in the crash taking the title of "baby projectile". When I finally arrived in Ohio, my invisible protectors followed me and oversaw my battle with scarlet fever. Shortly thereafter, Mom got a good scare when a bottle of baby powder I was holding, as she changed my diaper, dumped onto my face nearly choking me to death. I was definitely meant to be here!

Many details of the next few years are vague. Mom and Dad had somewhat of a relationship. I'm not sure what to call it. Mom was trying to be independent and Dad stayed with his parents on and off. He kept himself busy with things like photography, building motorcycles, and put a lot of importance on personal transcendence and meditation. And then there were other hobbies that were not as constructive. My father was an extremely handsome young man with beautifully long, silky and flowing brown hair with deep blue eyes that attracted a lot of ladies. Though his mother urged him to settle down with Sharon and his newborn, the free spirit in him prevented that. Rather than sticking it out in law school, he decided to take on the lucrative business of drug dealing, started carrying a gun, and made friends in all the wrong places.

Dad never got much support, especially from his mother, on a financial or emotional level and this led him to act out in a way that any rebellious kid would do. Of course, one can't blame their parents for everything. Some of it was the era. The 1960's were drastically changing times filled with a new generation trying to break away from the old ways of thinking. Dirty politics, murder, scandal and the Vietnam war were raging in the midst of flower power and the age of Woodstock. The 'in thing' was to transcend your mind and share love freely. It all sounded good until drugs were added to the mix. How unfortunate! It would've been interesting to see how far this great movement would have gone. My parents were caught up in all of this as they played games with one another, not realizing that this baggage was being passed down to their child.

While Mom's time was consumed with a baby, Dad had plans to go to Woodstock with a date and a couple of buddies, driving in his Cadillac hearse. They were on their way to attend a three-day concert that would go down in history. There were thousands of people and the roads were completely jammed. It seemed impossible to get his vehicle even remotely close to the site, and then Dad's buddy, Eddie, got a bright idea. Driving around in a hearse was obviously unusual, though morbidly funny and a bit rock-star-ish. As they approached a standstill, Eddie put on his top hat and hung himself out the window exclaiming, "Make way! Jefferson Airplane is here! Make way!" And like Moses parting the Red Sea, an opening was made and Dad got front row parking. They rolled out of the smoke-filled hearse laughing their asses off. The entire experience was extraordinary for those free spirits and it would set the benchmark for future generations.

Sharon was home learning to be a mother and doing a lot of soul searching. She was a beautiful, petite young girl with long brown hair, hazel eyes, and a smile that lit up a room. Even with a baby, guys were paying attention to her. Her mother, Zofie, had been wrong after all! Sharon loved music and enjoyed singing. She was sweet, sensitive, and expressed herself most effectively on paper through letters and poetry. Mom always seemed her best when she was in love. But during that time, she was heartbroken, confused and extremely pissed at Leif. Zofie had her back. Grandma didn't like my long-haired hippie Dad or his mother, for that matter. In fact, she couldn't stand either of them. On one occasion, Dad went to her house and sat with his legs spread, sporting holes in his blue jeans including his crotch. Grandma Zofie, with her wonderfully distinctive Polish accent said to Sharon, "Tell Dat Sanny Claus to shut his legs!" She couldn't help but think that Leif was bad news and she gave her daughter tons of support. Mom decided to play the field and shop for a man. Why should she sit around while Leif's out with God knows who? Well, she found one all right. His name was Lenny.

In the meantime, Rita continued to hound her son to do the right thing and ask Sharon to marry him. He caved and finally agreed, but by now the damage was done and the game playing went into overtime. Sharon didn't believe he was sincere, partly because of Rita's strong efforts to get them together. She thought, "Why would he need his mother to talk him into committing? I'll show HIM!" Driven by ego, she would marry Lenny because he seemed to care and pay attention to her and her daughter. Leif then responded by marrying another woman he'd been hanging around with for a while. Mom wasn't surprised. She was a cute brunette with puppy dog eyes which gave her a sexy, sleepy look. It wasn't a wonder that he was totally enamored with her.

Here I was, in the middle of it all; the little thing that tied my parents together. Somehow there remained a love between the two of them that kept their friendship afloat. I went back and forth with visitation and my step-mom didn't seem to mind my mother's presence. Lenny, on the other hand, turned out to be an extremely jealous man and became quite possessive and controlling with my mother. Consumed with fits of rage, his tantrums were so childish that he felt the need to scribble out my father's name on anything he saw. Once, as my father stood outside waiting to see me and speak with Mom, Lenny picked me up and held me out the second story window, threatening to drop me as he argued with my mother. Now his true colors were coming to light and she lived in fear. To spend time together as a family, my parents would secretly plan to meet at the park to talk and go for long strolls. What had she gotten herself into? Lenny was a nightmare! She adored Leif and now felt she had made a critical mistake.

It's times like these when our faith must be at its strongest when searching for solutions. Sometimes problems take care of themselves. Lenny decided to rob a number of banks and talked one of Mom's friends into joining him. Eventually they were caught, and Sharon found herself visiting her friend in federal prison. Lenny escaped and fled to Hawaii where he murdered someone before being apprehended and sentenced to twenty years. Mom was granted a divorce and was finally free of him.

Enjoying her freedom, Mom took me to Chicago, made some friends, and got the bug to travel around the country with a band. One of the guys expressed interest in my mother's singing and writing abilities, though I'm sure he was interested in much more. She thought this could be her big break and the chance to go out and make something of herself. Supposedly, she sang backup vocals on one of their albums, but I never heard it. What I know for sure is that she left me behind in the temporary care of my dad and step-mom who were back in Wisconsin, until my mother's parents, Zofie and Loosha, filed for legal guardianship and took me back to Ohio to avoid my being given away.

As the months went by and things were not working out for her on the road as she had hoped, Sharon envisioned coming home. She felt guilty for leaving me and ashamed for making another bad decision. Christmas was coming around again and she didn't want to return empty handed, so she agreed to take part in an illegal activity to make some quick cash. One of the guys stole a checkbook and they went up and down the eastern portion of the country, sending my mother into the banks to cash bad checks. I don't know how much money they stole, but it was enough to get her home. As she entered the threshold, she loosened her laces and removed her shoes to quietly walk through the house, nervously making her way to the familiar voices in the living room. She wondered if I would even recognize her as she rounded the corner and stood in the doorway, watching me play on the floor. Her stomach was in knots as she held her breath when I turned to see her. "Mama!" I said, in love and amazement. She rushed to embrace me with tears of joy and relief in her eyes. I had not forgotten her.

Mom stayed close to home, socializing and partying as she continued to search for herself. This time she would bring me along to some of the hippie gatherings and motorcycle blessings where there were all types of drugs and naked people floating around. I was introduced to a vast array of interesting characters; one of which included a biker chick running for her life from the president of a gang in California after being discovered that she was stealing money. A few folks seemed WAY out there, lost in the rambling waves of inebriation. Others were calm and cool soul-searchers just chilling out to pass the time. Mom's laughter confirmed her well-being and she was relaxed, but the past tends to creep up on us when we least expect it. Somehow, some way, the bad karma we create always makes certain that all our debts are paid one way or another.

One day, Sharon decided to visit her friend in jail who robbed the bank with her ex. When she arrived to check in, they informed her that since he was in a federal prison, she needed special permission to visit. They made her wait in a room and when the officers returned they threw down a stack of checks with her fingerprints all over them, accompanied by her face on a number of bank surveillance photos. Busted! Now she was off to jail and I remained in the care of my grandparents for the next few years.

While she did her time in a couple of southern women's prisons, she had plenty of time to reflect upon her life. Once, she witnessed someone's throat being cut. The aggressor put her finger to her lips as a warning to say nothing. Sharon did just that. Instilled with fear for her life, she withdrew and wrote letters and poetry to pass the time. She thought about her poor decision making as she spoke with jail counselors and participated in some of the programs offered. She thought about me and wanted to straighten herself out. She thought about my dad and six months after my fourth birthday, Mom received a telegram in jail briefly stating that Leif was dead.

Throughout my childhood, I was told many versions of the story. "Your Dad had a heart attack." "He was sick and lying on his back as he choked in his own vomit." "He and his wife threw a party and when he was overdosing, everyone got scarred and left him to die." "A buddy of his brought over some heroin. His wife got pissed off and left the house for hours as the two guys hung out. Later that day, he retired to his room, lay on his back in his waterbed and succumbed to an overdose." Any way I look at it, he did it to himself.

I remember my mother's parents, Grandma Zofie and Grandpa Loosha, carrying me across a busy street to the front of a white building before setting me down. Holding my hand as we entered the funeral parlor, we walked up a set of stairs leading to a large, open room on the left. All eyes stared at me as I scanned the room and saw my father sleeping. Slowly, I approached the casket, stood on my tiptoes to peer in, saw what he was wearing, and noticed that I couldn't see the lower half of his body. I later found out that only half the casket was opened because he was bare foot; the way he liked to be. A man crouched down to get to my level, looked me in the eyes, and gave me two flowers. I held them in my little hands and stared down at them as he said a few words that I can no longer recall. I heard Grandma Rita thanking Zofie and Loosha for bringing me before we left. I imagine my step-mom was there, though I can't see her in my mind. Within the next couple of years, she made the newspaper for being involved in buying product to supply a drug lab to make speed with her friends.

I always wanted to run into her again to have a chat, a moment of healing, and a time for forgiveness. My father's sister told me not to waste my time looking for her, "She won't give you the truth anyways. The woman is pure evil. I never understood what my brother saw in her." Recently explaining more of the story, she told me, "One of their friends gave Leif a painting of the devil. It was the creepiest thing I ever saw and they hung it in their front hallway. There was something about it that wasn't right. It was pure evil just like her." Then she recalled the day my father died. "It was most unusual. First, she called the house and then she came over which was something she NEVER did, saying she thought something was wrong with Leif. Your grandparents and I got in the car and took what seemed to be the longest car ride ever. I just knew something horrible had happened." There was a look of repulsion on my aunt's face as she remembered seeing him on his back. She chose not to give me gory details but only said that it was absolutely awful. I had no idea that she and my grandparents found him like that. What a terrible memory to carry around, not to mention the disbelief and anger attached to it. They, as well as my mom, always blamed my step-mother and thought she was cheating on Dad with the heroin seller. I would love to hear her side of the story. The whole thing seemed shady, but I don't expect to ever know the whole truth.

Shortly after Dad died, Mom was released from prison and we were reunited in the year of my fifth birthday. I have a strong recollection of her buttoning up my shirt in Grandma's kitchen, saying, "Oh boy! First day of school!" I was thankful she was there for that. We stayed at her parent's house until I finished the first grade. Mom found a nice boyfriend and that's when she decided we should get our own apartment. The place was only five minutes away from Grandma's and she was itching to get out on her own again. This time she felt more prepared.

In reflection: I have spent years trying to extract the truth about the far past, as I thought it would help me to understand the dysfunction of my life. Many details about my first six years seemed sketchy and filled with fabricated stories to dismiss the questions of a child. I carried around a lot of anger because of what other people told me as truth, in their opinion. There were no options to believe any differently and later, when everyone's stories started to change, I felt deluded. I started forming my own opinions and beliefs. I became distrustful of people even if they were genuinely honest. The positive side to that was street smarts. So, I'm thankful. This part of my life taught me self-awareness which was the first and most important step to repairing the holes in myself.

CHAPTER 2

GROWING ROOTS

ZOFIE AND LOOSHA, MY beloved guardian grandparents, were an intriguing couple. Both had very strong character which led them to clash frequently, filling the house with constant bickering, (mostly in Polish to protect my ears). They had separate bedrooms and never vacationed together, though they did have a certain tolerant love for one another that surfaced on occasion, usually at a social gathering or while watching a TV show.

Both had endured severe hardship while growing up at a time when there was no electricity or gas available in homes. They survived the Great Depression and experienced the years of Prohibition. Those times were true character builders and it's no wonder a lot of people grew to be hard, authoritative disciplinarians. My mother and her brother told me stories about their childhood and what Loosha and Zofie were like in those days. True old-school discipline was at its best. Their home sported a 'Pida' or better known in the English language as a cat of nine tails. This little homemade stick with long leather straps would literally whip your ass good! My mother told me that she and her brother used to hide these beasts because they hurt like hell! If their parents couldn't find it, another one was hand-made and Mom chuckled as she recalled, "One day, your grandma was cleaning and found a WHOLE PILE of whips hidden in the entryway bench seat!"

Another occurrence Mom's brother mentioned seemed unbelievable to me. My uncle sat innocently on the floor in front of the television and Grandpa walked by, reached out and ripped a pinch of hair out of his head. Such nonsensical moments like that were a regular occurrence for him. He would be scarred for the rest of his life. Tensions in the house were common and arguments between Loosha and Zofie rarely ceased. The arguments escalated to the point that Grandpa held a knife to Grandma's throat. Total chaotic dysfunction! Most of these truths were hidden from me until I was a teenager and I am thankful for that.

Those stories were pure fiction to me. Grandpa NEVER threatened or hurt me! I have witnessed my grandparent's anger with one another though. One time, Grandma was fuming mad and looked around for something to throw at him. When she saw nothing, she took her own teeth out and whipped them at him. It was like watching a crazy cartoon, cracking me up every time, and leaving me laughing hysterically! I'm sure that over time, they realized their mistakes and felt guilty about how they disciplined their children because they treated me like gold. I absolutely idolized them!

Loosha was born in Canada in 1914. His parents were passing through from Poland, making their way to the United States. He had six sisters and, though I don't know much about his boyhood, he told me a few things. He and a buddy used to pack a lunch, hop a freight train and disappear for days, hanging their food packs from the roof so that the mice and rats couldn't get into it. Like most people of the time, he dropped out of school to go to work. His mother treated him royally because he gave her half of his pay. Grandpa made twenty-nine cents an hour at a steel plant and, during the Depression, was lucky to get two or three days a week. He gave me some interesting facts that seemed unheard of. Beer was five cents for an 8-ounce glass, milk was seven cents a quart, pay phones were five cents, doctor visits were two bucks, and bread was eight cents a loaf. There weren't many apartments, which went for ten bucks a month, including utilities. There were outhouses until the 1930's when plumbing finally came around and travel was mostly done by streetcar for ten cents a ride. If you traveled out of the train station by way of railcar, it would only cost a buck fifty. There was no such thing as pizza and wings. There were no supermarkets and you had to buy food at the farmers market. Drinking was illegal during the Prohibition years after World War I and Grandpa told me about some of the speakeasies in the city, which were illegal drinking nightclubs. "You'd go at night and say a password something like, 'Joe sent me'." There were illegal bookie joints, gambling houses and prostitution rings. Grandpa called them hustlers and streetwalkers. I didn't ask if he partook in the activities, but he told me exactly where the Cinderella Inn and the Crystal Inn were located.

Television didn't come until the 1940's, so radio programs like "The Shadow" and "Twenty Thousand Years in Sing Sing" were popular along with a radio announcer named Tokyo Rose. Silent movies were available and were mostly love stories and westerns. The hot music of the day was hillbilly, swing and blues.

Everything Grandpa Loosha told me was fascinating. I recall him working for an oil company as a welder and foreman. During the holidays, Grandpa discovered his guys sneaking around making Christmas tree stands for themselves, thinking, "They won't finish the job on time!" He decided to call a meeting and told them, "Today you make Christmas tree stands and tomorrow we work." He had never seen them work harder and the job was completed in plenty of time! In the heat of summer, he sent one of the men out to get ice cream for the gang. He was an S.O.B. at times, but because of his actions and fairness, he was well respected. I wanted to be just like him!

Most of my personal memories had to do with Grandpa's professional photography business and retirement. He had a studio set up in the basement with a dark room. I was amazed as he let me transfer the photo paper from one tray of chemical to another, watching the picture magically appear in the red lit room. Such an intelligent and skilled man! He designed and built my uncle's house out in the country and made homemade wine from the Concord grapes he grew there. I remember the wine press and huge glass containers for distilling and always had a lot of questions as I shadowed him. While Grandma Zofie was at work, Grandpa and I hung out and he took me everywhere. I suppose he had to. In his retirement, he was the daytime babysitter, but if he minded, he certainly didn't show it. We really enjoyed each other's company and he called me his 'silent partner' as I was involved with many of his projects. Well …mostly I observed, but he made me feel like I was helping him. When we were in the truck, I watched him drive in admiration and grabbed my imaginary steering wheel so that I could drive with him. I shadowed every left, every right, or change of hand position on the steering wheel. His hardy laugh overpowered the radio as he looked at me and said, "Maybe I should install one for you on your side of the dash board!"

I have so many fond memories of Grandpa Loosha. Learning to play chess on the living room floor, fishing and visiting with his sisters was always fun, but there were a couple things that really stood out. Sometimes, I would babysit HIM! One evening, my grandmother went out to Bingo and when she returned home and walked into the parlor (as we called it then), she couldn't believe her eyes as she giggled. Often, Grandpa grabbed a throw pillow from the couch and lay on the floor on his side in front of the TV. Usually, he dozed off and on that particular night, I thought he was cold and wanted to tuck him. I crawled over to the side of his armchair to a pile of newspapers and carefully took apart each sheet. One by one, from head to toe, I covered him up. When Grandma walked into the parlor, she saw me sitting quietly in his rocking chair watching TV as loud snoring sounded from within a huge mound of newspaper in the middle of the room. I'm sure she gave him an ear full that night, but luckily, I was a good kid and didn't find much trouble. I used Grandma's lipstick a few times to explore my creative side and color the heat registers but that was about it.

Grandma Zofie had a sense of humor but didn't find Grandpa funny at all, though she did enjoy laughing AT him! She told me about a time when I was a toddler and he dropped me off at my cousin's house early before work. It was a frigid winter and he carefully carried me towards the house across the icy pavement as I nibbled on an apple. He slipped and wiped out as my favorite snack went flying but managed to hold on tightly to prevent my hitting the ground. Grandma's eyes were filled with joyful tears when telling me that, even though he fell and hurt himself, all I could say was, "My appo! My appo!" She was absolutely hysterical!

Grandpa Loosha did a lot of funny things; at least in my mind he did. Grandma Zofie was rarely impressed with him. He loved to wear his worn-out T-shirts that were riddled with holes or stains. He farted loudly, very often, and had fun with it. Grandma would be stirring something on the stove as he'd walk behind her and let one go. His eyes would widen and he'd say with a surprised look on his face, "Did you say something?" She would get pissed and mumble at him. A minute later he'd do it again, look at me and say, "Watt'd dat asshole say?" I couldn't contain myself! He was so incredibly playful, and grandma didn't GET IT!

He loved to make me laugh and loved even more to get under Grandma's skin in attempts to try and soften her up. It didn't work very often but every day he tried. I recall coming home from the farm and Grandma getting supper started; usually some Polish dish like pierogi or golumpki (pigs in a blanket). The three of us would sit down to eat and they would talk a little bit about the day. Grandpa Loosha, with his big belly, grey-blue eyes, bushy brows, and humor on board, began making dramatic slurping noises as he sipped his coffee. Grandma shot him the 'look' and continued to eat her supper, aggravated. He looked at me with a smile and did it again. It was no wonder they always argued. He was constantly instigating! As usual, he sat at the table with his disheveled Fruit of the Loom T-shirt, and during our meal he would wipe his face down his sleeve. Grandma exclaimed, "Swinia!" (This is Polish for pig). She'd start making fun of his eyebrows. "You look like a big monster wit doze bushes on yer head. Why doan you shave dem and look like a normo human being!"

Inside, I was glowing with delight because frankly, I thought he was hysterical and I loved those big grey eyebrows! It tickled me to see Grandma pick on him. Again, he looked at me and chuckled with wide eyes telling me, "Watch this!" He purposely rubbed his face on his sleeve and wiped his hands down the front of his chest over his big belly before returning his elbows to the table. Grandma drew a big sigh, gazed into her dinner plate, and just mumbled again. This would go on for years! Her reactions amused me every time.

In reflection: Grandpa Loosha was like a big, happy clown entertaining me. What I failed to see at the time was that he was teaching me about self-love. It doesn't matter what other people think of you. They will always judge and try to change you, even your own spouse. He showed me how to be unique and not to let others get me down. Laughter and light-heartedness is the key. He was my beloved jokester and major influence in my life. I thank him for so much, especially my sense of humor!

Grandma Zofie was a cosmetologist who started in her basement, later growing into a full-blown business after riveting airplanes during the second World War. When she was a kid, she grew up on a large farm with six brothers and five sisters. She shared a few rough stories with me about how it was back then; like walking many miles to school in deep snow with no boots or coat, working in the fields, and slaughtering the livestock they raised for meat. She described her father as "strict" and her mother as "an angel" who both immigrated from Poland. The family grew their own food, sold the rest at the farmers market, and Grandma said her mother churned the BEST sweet cream butter. "Da people bought it up as soon as day arrived on dare horse drawn carts!"

Grandma only made it to the sixth grade because the farm work was more important. Medicine wasn't up to par in her time. Her five-year-old brother bled to death after stepping on a piece of wood as he was being chased by a goose. One by one, each of her siblings grew up and left the farm, making Grandma's chores even more back breaking. One Easter Sunday, the house burnt to the ground and they were forced to live in the barn with the animals until they rebuilt.

There wasn't much entertainment, just constant work under the supervision of a slave driving father. On occasion, a neighbor would drop by and give her father a bottle of beer. Grandma Zofie always looked forward to this because she knew that when he finished it, he would take a nap in the haystack or underneath a tree. This meant, she and a couple of her sisters could sneak off to visit friends on nearby farms. Of course, if they got caught, they would be brutally beaten, so they were very careful not to do it too often. All the kids were fearful of their father. One time, during a typical day of chores, Zofie readied the horse to plow the fields. He stepped on her foot and it swelled up so bad that she could barely walk. She continued with her chores and kept this from her father, in fear that she would be whipped. Grandma suffered in silence for weeks.

The winters on the farm were bitter cold and several feet of snow bombarded the landscape. Grandma's father regularly sent her into the woods with an axe in the freezing weather, even though she had no winter coat, to chop wood for fuel to keep the house warm. Zofie impressed her father by always doing what she was told, and he considered her to be the best worker on the farm. Because of this, he promised to get her a coat but, being the tyrant that he was, she never got it.

When she turned sixteen, she finally stood up to him. Her father was in a fit of rage, yelling and screaming as he came at her mother and knocked some pots off the coal stove, dumping the contents to the floor. Grandma Zofie knew her mother had been working on it all day and she also knew that her mother would not stand up for herself. Grandma stepped in front of him to defend her mother and told him off for the first time in her life. He raised his fist, broke her nose, and she left the farm never to return. Her father went to the local judge to try and get her back, but Zofie was of age and there was nothing he could do. For maybe the first time in his life, he cried. He died soon after on an Easter Sunday and the farm was sold. In later years, grandma would only talk about the farm if I asked and she always ended with, "I would naver go back! Not even fur a million dollars!"

My earliest memories of Grandma Zofie are with Bingo. She played Bingo at every local Catholic church just about every night of the week. I accompanied her hundreds of times, even before I could actually play. Boy did she love to gamble! In fact, most Catholics seemed to enjoy gambling and I was in training! We'd always arrive at the Bingo hall at least an hour prior to start time so we could get that 'lucky seat' in a 'special section' that she preferred. She and her friends would save seats for each other by placing a Bingo board faced down on an empty spot. An admission board was purchased for a dollar and you paid fifty cents each for extras boards, but it was important to only buy a couple at the door! Oh …and only a couple of paper specials too! You see, there's a certain strategy in trying to find those lucky cards! There are folks that walk around with aprons selling extra boards and specials. Grandma said it was important to get a variety from the different sellers to mix it up a bit. Once settled in our seats, then came the set up. The handy Bingo stick was pulled out, which is a piece of wood that is split in half and joined at the center with a hinge for easy fold-up and storage under the car seat. A long groove is routed in the top of the stick, perfectly sized to hold upright your first row of Bingo boards and allowing more to be propped on the bottom edge of the stick, giving you two long rows of serious Bingo playing! Grandma usually played ten to twelve cards and I would watch her set up. Her purse was strategically placed behind the upright cards along with the little white garbage pails. The Bingo game schedule was always placed next to her and she would start checking her numbers to see how many of the seventy-five she had. If there were a lot missing, it was necessary to buy a couple more boards.

Now for the paper specials. Each book had to be pulled apart and sorted according to color and placed in the correct order of play. Occasionally, a glue stick was used to tack the specials together and create a full page that didn't slip when using the ink dabber to stamp the numbers called. Grandma's purse was equipped with every color of ink dabber available at the time. Now that we were settled, it was time to dip into the pile of extra cash on the table for soda pop, pretzels, chips, and pizza. This was always my favorite part. Some Bingo halls even sold homemade cheese pierogi during intermission that was an absolute MUST after the crowd's mad dash to the restroom.

I remember the first-time she bought me an admission board. I was the only five-year-old gambling in the place! I was so excited to be REALLY playing next to my Grandma and thought, "Someday I will play as many cards as her!" As the numbers were called she would cover her own first and then look at mine to make sure I didn't miss any. I don't remember winning in those infant Bingo years, but I do remember the jolt of anxiety if I needed one more number to win, followed by terrible disappointment when it wasn't called. Later, I graduated when Grandpa Loosha made me my very own fold-up Bingo stick that I proudly stored under the car seat next to Grandma's.

Once a week, my grandparents and I would go to "the farms" where my uncle's house was built. This was the same area where my grandma grew up and it was a beautiful drive. We listened to country music on the truck radio as I studied and memorized the landmarks en-route to our destination. My uncle owned half the property and my grandparents owned the other half, which had a barn, grapes, and a large veggie garden. Upon arrival every Saturday morning, the first stop was the barn. Grandma fetched the rakes, hoes, and bushel baskets while Grandpa hopped on the old tractor and headed over to the vineyard. I always wanted to go with him for a ride but most times had to stay and help Grandma work the soil. I can still smell the fresh, clean, damp morning country air, and hear the choir of crickets, birds and frogs. The feel of the dirt and occasional waft of cow dung from another farm up the road filled me with a peace I could not yet identify. Later in the morning, I anticipated dropping the work and running off to play with my first cousins. When they awoke, they would run from the house down to the garden to meet me. This was my "get out of jail free" card.

In Reflection: spending a few of my early years with my grandparents gave me a bit of a solid foundation to build on. Thank God that they took me in and cared for me. I sometimes wondered if Grandma Zofie signed papers of legal guardianship just to cover up her daughter's mistakes, save some embarrassment, and earn more respect with her gossipy sisters and beauty salon clientele. I can't imagine anyone wanting to take on that great a responsibility so late in life. She and Loosha really committed themselves to me; something they forgot to do with their own children. Was this another chance? A chance to change some of the dysfunction? Whatever it was, they did a good job. They were my home, my world, my heart and soul, my teachers, protectors, and caregivers. These are the days I hold closest to my core that created a longing in my heart to be 'home'. I would get the chance to return the favor, much later.

My father's parents, Rita and Teddy, were very different from my mother's side. Grandpa Teddy was a well-dressed, calm, cool, and collected man while Grandma Rita was a constant nag and quite pushy. They owned a bar and usually resided in gated communities with access to golf courses, bike paths, tennis courts, and private inground swimming pools. They owned a summer cottage in Canada which brings back memories of playing with my father in the yard and building sand castles on the beach.

They taught me about the importance of manners and always encouraged my artistic and problem-solving abilities by providing lots of puzzles and advanced coloring books. They took me to theatrical plays, museums, and taught me how to cross-country ski. Both of them were active and took me for many bicycle rides, walks, and games of catch in the yard. I admired their interesting home with a bear skin rug in front of the fireplace and a Civil War musket hanging over the mantel. Grandpa's carved tobacco pipes rested on the coffee table, lit by captivating lamps and stained-glass screens. Their home was warm and comfortable with big soft beds and heavy down comforter's that swallowed you up and made it easy to fall asleep. The smell of eucalyptus leaves and freshly picked flowers always aroused my senses.

Rita and Teddy traveled all over the world and once took me along to Hawaii, but Grandma Rita always insisted that they didn't have money. "We were in the bar business, you know. We struggled!" This was always a common statement when she didn't want to help financially. My mom told me that Dad used to steal money from the bar cash register because his parents wouldn't give him any, or at least not enough. Grandma was a control freak and used money to bargain my father into cutting his hair and then would not pay up. When he needed money while away at school, she would only give him the bare minimum. She stressed the importance of education and my father was tested and proved genius as he entered college at age sixteen to study law. And yet, Rita constantly lectured her brilliant son, all the while putting down his beliefs and dreams. No wonder her children were rebellious!

All my life, she did the same to me. She never stopped nagging and trying to impose her ideals on me. She thought the clothes I wore were unacceptable and blamed my other grandmother. They despised one another and argued over me frequently. Zofie "Dressed me like a farmer," according to Rita or 'Sweetie' as she made me call her. Zofie argued that Rita "Dressed me like a D P." (That means Displaced Person: a term used to describe immigrants arriving from a foreign country). And I DID feel that way. When 'Sweetie' bought me dresses and clothes with loud patterns and bright colors, I was extremely uncomfortable and felt embarrassed.

Although my Grandmothers were like oil and water, Loosha and Teddy steered clear of the drama. Both were so wise and easy going and they certainly showed respect by giving these women plenty of room! I could never understand how Grandpa Teddy did it. Out of pure annoyance, I said to him once, "How can you live with her? How have you put up with this for all these years?" My comment reflected the ongoing nagging in the car. "Teddy slow down! Teddy the light is turning red. Teddy put your blinker on. Teddy! Teddy! Teddy!" Numerous other times, when he and I were having a moment and discussing life, she would chime in with the argument, "Teddy, that's not what you should be telling her!" Everything he said to me made perfect sense. He defended himself on occasion but her knack for talking over other people always gave her the last word.

In later years, I began to understand why Grandpa stuck it out. When she was young, Rita took care of all her brothers and sisters while her parents worked. I'm sure this had everything to do with her strong will. Rita's driving force was the only reason why anything got done. When Grandpa Teddy developed throat cancer, had his voice box removed, went through chemotherapy and radiation, his spirits were at an all-time low. Grandma pushed him hard with her nagging persistence and worked with him every day on his speech therapy. At first, he had one of those monotone mechanical devices to allow him to speak. With relentless practice, he learned to voice words on his own through a 'burping' method. Starting from the very beginning with ABC's, Rita pushed and encouraged him. After some time, he was quite good at speaking and lived out the rest of his life as a healthy man. He died when I was twenty-one and I lost Grandpa Loosha that year as well. It was devastating! I had lost two of the most positive male influences in my life.

I did a lot of reflecting that year, recalling the sound advice Grandpa Teddy always shared with me. I wish I could remember every word. My mind would travel back in time to when I was a teenager sitting at the dinner table. Grandpa Teddy had said, "You are a young lady that will grow into a sophisticated and successful woman if your choices are made carefully." These words resonate with me to this day.

I also found a new appreciation for Grandma Rita. After Grandpa passed, she lived independently in the south, staying active and keeping her mind sharp by reading and paying attention to current events. She still maintained some old-school opinions but showed better adaptation. She admitted to me that she blamed herself for not helping my father out more during his college years. "If I had just sent him more money, perhaps he wouldn't have looked for it elsewhere. Maybe if I had listened to him more, things would be different." For the first time in my life, I felt empathy for her. All those years, she had been carrying around a heavy load of guilt.

For the longest time, I did blame her for adding to my father's ultimate demise. But all in all, I learned to accept Grandma Rita for who she was and ignored the rest of the garbage. I traveled south to see her on occasion, but usually we talked on the phone. As I developed a better ability to "let go" and not "have to be right," conversations became pleasant and we could laugh and appreciate each other more. She was in her late nineties when she died. I hope that my father was the first to greet her.

In reflection: Both of my grandmothers were strong willed women that stood their ground and showed me the value of speaking up, taking action, putting up with NO bullshit, and doing things for yourself. I admire this and completely embrace it.

CHAPTER 3

NEW GROWTH

NOW THAT SHE WAS out of jail and again trying to get her head together, it was time for Sharon to take responsibility for her daughter and get an apartment. It was the mid-1970's and I had just finished the first grade. I had some anxiety about moving out of Grandma's house and changing schools, although I would have my own bedroom! I could decorate it as I wished and create my own personal and private place of escape for myself! This was very appealing.

Our new home was only a mile away from my grandparents. Grandma set us up with all the basic kitchen stuff: pots, silverware, dishes, and a table. Our dining room was empty with just a rug and a small desk. The living room had a wooden rocking chair and something resembling a couch with no back on it. Vinyl records and 8-track tapes were the latest thing and though we didn't have a tape player, we did have an all-in-one turn-table stereo unit. It had a hinged plastic cover over the record player which topped a radio receiver. Grandpa gave us a small black and white TV with rabbit ears to get better reception.

Cable TV and internet weren't invented yet and small hand-held transistor radios were the only portable source of entertainment. There were no remote controls. All electronics had knobs for everything! Turning up the volume and finding a station to watch or listen to meant getting off your ass and walking across the room. Head phones were huge ugly contraptions that weighed heavily on your head unless you had the 'in ear' bud (Yes, that's singular), made from hard plastic that never stayed in well. When I think of all this it's hard to believe! Even the telephone was ancient. No touch screens, just rotary. Cordless didn't exist. Phones stayed wherever they could plug into the 'jack' which was usually on the kitchen wall or in the living room. To get some privacy you could only walk as far away as the cord reached.

I grew to appreciate my new-found privacy. I loved my room and spent a lot of time there. Since computers weren't around, I had to be creative to keep myself busy with my stuffed animals and Matchbox cars. My dad's parents made me a dollhouse with furnishings that I constantly rearranged and it stirred my imagination of having my own real house with a tool shop like Grandpa Loosha someday. Santa Claus brought me a record player for my room that year. I loved listening and singing along to whatever was available in the house, but my favorites were Led Zeppelin, Fleetwood Mac, and The Beatles.

I adored animals and felt a special connection to them. I missed the golden retriever we had briefly at Grandma's house. His stay with us was short lived when he started pissing on her tomato plants. I was told he ran away but didn't believe it. I knew he wouldn't leave me. At my insistence of needing the truth, I found out that he was given away. It was the only time I was ever enraged with my grandparents. My mother must've sensed a longing in me because shortly after getting our apartment, a tabby tiger cat showed up. We named her Muffin, and she was so entertaining! I fell in love and she brightened my world. I couldn't help but laugh every time she napped and blended in with all the other stuffed animals on my bed.

House cats back then were practically unheard of and most were indoor/outdoor. On one of her adventures, she came home pregnant and I was so excited about it! Every day when I got home from school I asked my mother, "Did she have them yet?" I must have drove her crazy with my impatience! When the kittens finally arrived, I wanted to stay home from school to be with them. Every morning I'd say, "Mommy, I don't feel good," and it worked! But after a couple of times, she was on to me. Damn!

It was awesome to see my cat nurture five kittens, but also difficult to handle the fact that we couldn't keep them all. I went on a mission in my neighborhood to try and give them to people I knew so that I could still visit them. When Muffin came home pregnant again, my mother gave her the boot because she couldn't afford the upkeep. She knew how I would react, so she let me keep one of the male kittens. Shortly after that, she wanted to get rid of him because he was very nasty. I named him "Sneaky" because he would creep up on people, jump up and bite his victim in the ass. I wanted so much to be his buddy and cuddle with him, not believing that he would ever hurt me. Mom constantly warned me to keep my face away from his. Sure enough, one day, I lay on the floor nudging closely and he sank his teeth into my cheek. I gasped, held in my tears and ran to the bathroom to treat my wounds without Mom knowing. I knew if she found out, she'd give HIM the boot too!

One winter, Sneaky was struck by a car and Mom tried to break the news gently. As she read the devastation on my face, she tried to make it humorous by describing how he was frozen solid and had to be scrapped off the street. She placed his body in a box, but his tail stuck straight out of the top corner. The visual did make me laugh a little and I'm certain that my morbid sense of humor stems from that moment.

Santa Claus brought "Herbie", an orange tabby tiger cat, that year. Now this guy was a true buddy! I played with him constantly and he followed me everywhere. During a blizzard, I was sent to the store for some bread and supplies. Herbie watched as I bundled up in my snowsuit and he followed me outside to accompany me through the deep snow all the way to the store and back. I talked to him and laughed the whole way, feeling protected by him. In later years when I was in high school, he would sit on the porch and wait for me to come home late at night. We witnessed each other grow from tiny tots to adulthood. When I was out on my own after graduating from high-school, Mom found him dead in the driveway, just old and tired. I sobbed when hearing the news and wondered if he was waiting for me to come home. Even though my mom took care of him, I felt a sense of guilt that I had abandoned him when I moved out.

But let's rewind back to the days when Herbie and I were at our best together, because Mom and I were also at our best. These were the years that she and I were getting to know one another all over again. She certainly didn't want to spend any more time in jail and was now more aware of the importance of settling in and attempting to be a good mother. I remember the struggle. Sometimes she worked and other times she bought groceries with food stamps from the welfare department. There were times that she had to boil pots of water on the stove to pour into the tub to make a hot bath for me. The winter was so cold and getting out of bed to dress for school was hell! Mom would turn up the thermostat a little and tell me when it kicked on so that I could run right to the heat register and quickly get dressed in front of it while it blew precious warm air.

The half mile walk to school was just as much of a drag in bad weather. My boots were tall brown plastic tubes that zipped up to my kneecaps and kept my feet dry but the treads on the soles sucked, making it difficult to keep a good footing in the snow. The boys always seemed to have better gear like hiking boots, and I was a bit jealous. I wanted to wear pants like the boys too, instead of the required plaid dress uniform. My legs always froze in the winter and I thought it was very unfair. Years later, the parochial school system would finally make some changes and allow the girls to wear pants, but not soon enough for me!

I slowly became acquainted with my new neighborhood and made a few friends, staying within earshot of my mother's voice. There were a few girls I hung around with. One was more on the sporty side and enjoyed cheerleading. She taught me some of the lively moves and spirited chants, but it wasn't really fulfilling. I preferred playing the sports and being cheered ON rather than yelling from the sidelines. Two other neighborhood girls and I played board games and listened to music frequently. This was a little more my style. "Grease" was the new release and craze of the time and they loved acting out and singing the Olivia Newton John's parts of the movie. My favorite character was played by John Travolta, the tough guy in a black leather jacket. I participated in the reenactment, taking the tough guy part, but the girls vivaciousness always took over the show. Then, I met Jill. She was intimidating, very loud, bitchy and bossy for what seemed no apparent reason. And though she projected a dominant persona around a group of peers, she was fun when we were 'one on one'.

Jill represents the experience of wanting to be on "that girl's" team. For subconscious reasons, I wanted her as a friend rather than an enemy. She exhibited some sort of power that I thought I lacked and craved. "If I'm friends with her, others will respect and fear me." Looking back, all of this was in my mind. I was such a tomboy and being respected by others was never an issue. None the less, she persuaded me to say something mean to a girl. Deep down, I knew it wasn't right, but I wanted to please and impress Jill and did it anyways. This poor girl hung her head pouting and sobbing as she left my backyard, never to be seen again. Jill smiled with approval, and I laughed on the outside, but inside I was mortified and never forgave myself. I learned a valuable lesson that day: to trust my own judgement and always be kind.

Because of this, I smartened up and discovered there were parts of Jill that I just couldn't grow to like. The mouth and the attitude were way too intense for me. My seven-year-old mind began to re-evaluate itself and realized that it also possessed a little "know it all" (as most children do) and I started standing up to Jill, usually winning any disputes. I didn't give it much thought when she moved away but now realize how influential she was in the forming of my character and I am thankful.

In general, I preferred to play with the boys on the street. They were way more entertaining! Football, street hockey, baseball, it didn't matter. I kicked ass and developed a reputation, of which I was unaware of, for being "that girl" who played with the boys and had their respect as a competitor. Tough girl? You bet! I didn't need Jill's protection after all! I created my own by just being myself. And so, with the boys, I was in my element with the activity, discovery, and trouble. This leads me to CJ.

When Mom and I first moved into the neighborhood, I rode my bicycle on the sidewalk from one corner to the other repeatedly. And though my body was small, my imagination was larger than life. First, I was a traveler from a far-off land exploring this unfamiliar landscape. Then, I was a biker like my dad and my mom's boyfriend, cruising on my obnoxiously loud Harley Davidson with the wind in my hair. As I pedaled faster, I morphed into a motocross racer, gripping tightly as I conquered the rough terrain, jumping the cracks in the sidewalk; totally unaware of my audience. CJ, soon to be my first real friend on the block, and his friend were watching the race with awe and curiosity. Who was this girl? How fast is she going? Will she let us join? They decided to add to the obstacle course, laying on the grass while holding their hockey sticks across the sidewalk. As I rode through a couple times, smiles brightly lit their faces as I drove over their speed bumps, making the sticks click and clang against the ground. Onward now to the corner and back. My chest rose as I took in the adrenaline rush, "This time I will go as fast as I can!" Feverous momentum and determination kicked in as I approached, making eye contact and exchanging a devilish smile with CJ. My tires delivered a mighty blow and trampled over their trap, forcing their hands to let go of the violently bouncing and vibrating sticks. Ooo's and aahh's followed by laugher filled the air and the ice was broken. We introduced ourselves and parted ways in the hopes of seeing each other soon. And we did, day after day playing in the street, becoming joined at the hip.

    CJ had his friends and I had mine. He went to public school and I went to Catholic school. He was a bad boy and I was a good girl. Or was it, I was a bad girl and he was worse? Whatever the case, we saw eye to eye. He liked my ideas and I liked his attitude. We tore apart a busted-up fence from an abandoned house and used it to build a fort/clubhouse in my yard. (Perhaps an inspiration from spending time with Grandpa Loosha). There, we peeked at dirty pictures I found in my house and we played doctor, learning about ourselves. A boy married me and CJ and we carved a heart with our initials into the tar street with a pocket knife in front of my house. Ahh …puppy love!

    My mother once recalled grounding me from playing outside and I cried for CJ as I stood and stared out the window like a cat, wishing to be out there. But all good things were coming to an end soon. He would betray me by giving away our precious secrets to all his friends and my mother's new boyfriend would move us away. But wait. Let's not go there yet.

Mom's steady boyfriend was very cool in my book! He was a Navy Reserve guy that built his own trike (a three-wheel motorcycle) that was loud, fast, and pretty cool looking. I used to really enjoy it when he would pick me up from school when I was in the first grade. He revved the engine as I approached the bike and grabbed my helmet. All the kids and their parents were watching, and I had the feeling of true power as I fastened my own helmet buckle, climbed up on the seat and straddled the bike, tucking the front of my uniform dress under my inner thighs. I felt so good! So alive! I loved riding with him and was hooked on the energy rush that ran through my bones as the bike took off!

This guy was so interesting to me. I looked up to him. I wanted to join the Navy and be like him. I knew my mom loved this man and that made me happy. We went to concerts, motorcycle blessings, camping, beaches, and family functions together. These were the happiest days of my childhood and the best times I would have with my mother. We were pals, playing board games, laughing, and feeding our inner spirits. We carried each other through rough times, especially when the Navy man left us when I was about eight years old. We trusted one another and worked as a team. I went door to door for her during the winter season, selling homemade Christmas candleholders she and a friend made to create some extra cash. They drilled a hole halfway through the center of a nicely cut branch and secured feet on the bottom so that it wouldn't roll. They finished it off with red ribbon and pine needles surrounding a green or red candlestick. It turned out to be a great marketing move to send a little girl out door to door. The look of surprise and excitement lit their faces every time I proudly walked through the door with another empty box. They couldn't make them fast enough! When we didn't have money, Mom would always think of something and I admired her creativity and enjoying the simple things. This made all the difference in the world. It made it possible to get through anything with love in our hearts.

I remember one time when she didn't have a car and I towed her on my three-speed bicycle all the way home from Grandma's house. I never heard her laugh so hard in my life and I was so happy to be the one who made it happen. And though I feared her anger and discipline, which was usually a grab by the hair and a slap across the face, this didn't occur too often; only when I sassed back or worried her sick. I was trusted and treated as an adult. It was normal for me to light a cigarette on the gas stove for her while she got out the cigar box and separated the seeds and stems from her green herb before rolling a joint or two. I held the cigarette end over the flame, careful only to burn the tip and not start the middle of it on fire. One time, I got curious and put my lips on the filter to lightly draw smoke in my mouth and watch the tip glow before carrying it to my mother in the next room. She would never know! Or so I thought. I gave her the cigarette and went back to the kitchen.

Five seconds later, a stern, authoritative voice stated my full name and asked if I took a puff. I thought to myself, "How could she know?" Of course, I answered as any kid would, "No, Mom."

The voice in the next room showed no sign of being fooled, "Then how come the filter is wet?"

Oh crap! I didn't think of that! There's no getting out of this. I'm totally guilty! "I don't know," replied my quiet voice.

It was coming, wasn't it? The punishment, the stomping feet approaching quickly from around the corner carrying the monster head bearing bulging, bloodshot eyes filled with rage!

Nothing. Absolutely nothing! You can imagine my relief, but I don't remember ever being asked to light her smokes again. It wouldn't be until I turned thirteen or so that I would attempt smoking again. And those hand rolled smokes called "joints" that everyone wanted a "hit" off of …these were restricted to the adults only, but I was always allowed to participate in the rituals. Whether at a party with Mom at a friend's house, or in our own living room, I usually sat on the floor within the semi-circle gathering. As the sweet-smelling smoke filled the air, I enjoyed watching everyone interact. I felt I was a part of the tribe in my own quiet way, especially when I got to pass the joint from the person on my right to the person on my left. Never a puff, just a pass and I always got a "Thank you." Occasionally, I was addressed, asked questions, and was encouraged to join in the conversation.

My mother's friends had always shown a sort of love and care for me. These people were cheerful and positive, telling me to never forget that I was a good kid, special, smart, and as I grew up I would do great things. I looked up to them and they loved me. I saw no fault in them. I even forgave one of them for crawling into my bed and trying to get me to perform fellatio. He was extremely drunk, and I assumed that he thought he was in my mother's room. It was an uncomfortable experience to say the least. He had a smell to him, something I'd never smelled before and when I refused to open my mouth, he climbed on me and rubbed himself between my thighs as I lay on my stomach, pretending to be asleep. My six or seven-year-old mind thought, "So this is what Mom does in the other room?" Feeling very weird about the situation, I wanted to put an end to it as he was whispering to me. I moved my body away from him as much as I could and told him I needed a drink of water. His weight lifted, and I got out of bed as he followed me to the kitchen. He sat down at the table, looked up at me for a moment, put his hand to his face, and shook his head. It was then he realized who I was and that a terrible mistake had been made. I went back to my room and he did not follow. I was in disbelief over what just happened. And that dreadful odor! My bed smelled like it now! Great. I quickly moved to the edge of the bed when I discovered a small wet spot in the middle of the sheet and tried not to touch it as I stirred, trying to fall back asleep. I woke up to a dried crusty residue and wondered if my mother would notice when she did the laundry.

    I kept this to myself for many years and I'm not sure how this affected me. I wasn't hurt, just creeped out. CJ and I did similar things, though I don't remember if it was before or after this event. I did question whether I was normal or not. My sexual imagination had always been vivid and went as far back as I could remember. Long before Mom and I had the apartment, I had fantasies about my female kindergarten teacher. This followed me to the first grade when a cute young nun captured my attention. But nobody compared to my fourth-grade teacher! I thought about her for years. Liking boys was what all the girls did, so I did too, but I really liked girls more for some reason. I had a crush on one of my babysitters and looked forward to when Mom went out. I remember getting a little hyper around her, not knowing what to do with the feelings I had.

    There were a couple of girls I had the opportunity to experiment with on different occasions. I didn't see either of them very often but when we got together, we would sneak away and do some role-playing. I would always be the husband bringing home imaginary flowers and kissing her closed mouth. We giggled a lot and were careful not to get caught smooching. The other girl and I had sleep overs and pulled out the doctor kit that Grandma Rita bought me for Christmas. If she only knew what we did with that!

As I got older, I wondered how in the world I was so sexual at such a young age. The Catholic education gave me a sense of guilt and sinfulness, leaving me wondering if something was wrong with me. I tried putting the blame on my mother for taking me to crazy parties when I was a toddler, but really, there is no one to blame. Children discover themselves quite early and some are more insistent and exploratory than others. I was one of those early bloomers and unfortunately, was taught to feel dirty about it.

I recently had a conversation with a co-worker and she told me that when her son first discovered his penis he wouldn't leave it alone. Everywhere they went, his hand was in his crotch and she thought, "Oh no! I hope this doesn't become a problem." Another friend's daughter found that when she humped a pillow, stuffed animal, car seat, you name it, something really nice began to happen, so she tried to have these experiences as often as possible. From the beginning, our basic instinct isn't to procreate, but to feel good. No wonder some religions have gone overboard trying to keep this under control by using guilt.

At any rate, I never dared share any of my questions or adventures with my mother. Being the person that she was, it may have been ok, but when she found my diary and read about CJ, I was horrified and embarrassed. Boy, was I glad I didn't write about the girls in there! It was then I learned that if you don't want something known, DON'T write it down! But aside from that, Mom and I had lots of great conversations and I felt loved, safe, and important to her. I tried to make her proud, bringing home softball trophies and pitching "no-hitters" that became the talk of the entire Little League Softball club for years. I felt like a winner. I was a winner. And while I was basking in the beauty of it all, something dark was lurking around the corner. I was about to learn about true hatred, in the form of a man, who was about to poison all the good that existed in me, in my life, and in my relationship with my mother.

CHAPTER 4

LIGHTNING STRIKES

MOM HAD A FEW boyfriends that came and went. Some were nice and thoughtful. Some were creepy and others were just down right weird. She couldn't seem to find the right match after the Navy man. Then Mario started coming around. At first, he would show up on his bicycle and my mother was impressed that he was in good shape and peddled all that way to see her. After a while, he would pick her up in a hot sports car which impressed her even more. I guess the saying, "If you got a hot car, you get a hot girl," held true here. Mom was definitely a head turner and she could've had anyone she wanted, but her self-esteem had been too damaged to allow it. With all the 'bad luck' in the love category throughout the years, she now looked at things differently. This new guy made a good living, unlike any other she had given her time to. She craved a stable future with someone and wished to create a better life for me whether she was in love, or not.

These things became more apparent when he moved in with us. His home stereo system was unlike anything I'd ever seen with all kinds of separate components; equalizers, a receiver and a turntable that were quite remarkable, not to mention the huge speakers that filled the room with a concert-like experience. The collection of vinyl records was also impressive and he let me use his system to entertain my love for music. I would sit for hours at a time in Mom's wooden rocking chair spinning all kinds of tunes, listening to them very intensely and daydreaming the days away. Yes, I definitely liked the stereo! That first year when Mario was impressing Mom, Christmas was good too! I woke up to find the tree packed and stacked with presents and overflowing stockings, almost too heavy for the little nails they hung from over the fake fireplace. And it was ALL for me! Everything I asked from Santa was there and more!

All these material things being showered upon us was certainly a nice change. A shiny baited hook? Something didn't seem quite right to me, but mom didn't see it. I couldn't pin-point it, but something was wrong, and the feeling became stronger as the weeks passed. My behavior towards Mario changed and so did my attitude towards my mother. I wished for her to be happy. I wanted US to be happy, but she abruptly forgot about me and my thoughts. The first time I noticed this was when we were driving somewhere in his car. They were up front laughing and carrying on as I lay down in the back seat with a hell of a migraine. Headaches rarely paralyzed me but when they did, it was unbearable. The music was loud and I asked if they could please turn it off. I was ignored. The stabbing in my head made me cry and I was asked, "What's the matter?" As I explained and repeated my request, Mario's favorite song came on the radio. He cranked the volume to the max and it pounded a nail through my skull. I screamed in agony and covered my ears while trying to bury my head in the seat cushion. The obnoxious and wailing noise compounded by laughter claimed victory over my tears. Anger was born and quickly turned to resentment against both of them.

I understand that a single parent trying to find companionship would view their child's behavior as "adjustment time;" a certain "getting over" having to share mommy or daddy. Sometimes this is the case, but there was a certain selfishness my mother exhibited that was inexcusable. The very important bond she worked so hard to rebuild with me was becoming damaged again and unraveling just in time for my adolescence. We all know this is one of the most awkward, headstrong, confusing, and rebellious times that transform and fling us into adulthood. Do we pass with flying colors or do we become damaged goods that consume the rest of our adult lives, leading us to try and decipher what the hell is wrong? Most often, the latter is the case.

It would've been helpful to me if Mom kept the line of communication open and listened better to what I was trying to tell her. Instead, I was getting dumped with the babysitter more frequently. It was a blessing that I liked her so much. When I realized that Mario hated my beloved cat, Herbie, it became entirely clear that he was a shitty person. He tried winning me over with his gifts and told me that if I let him, he would adopt me. I didn't believe this to be sincere and my answer was a very abrupt "NO!" His words were what my MOTHER wanted to hear.

And so, she took the bait, hook, line and sinker. He moved us from our neighborhood to his. The place was only about twenty minutes away, but away from Grandma and Grandpa, away from my support system. To me, it seemed like the other side of the world. It was a two-bedroom house with a big yard and to Mom, it must have seemed perfect. Suburbia with a guy that made great money, put food in the fridge and paid the bills. No more food stamps and welfare cheese. Oh …and the weed. He was as fond of getting high as she was and now, it was always available and paid for. I would continue grade school in the parochial system. At least one thing would remain familiar …wearing a plaid uniform in the presence of religious figures. Ugh!

In the fall, I would begin sixth grade and in the meantime, my summer was spent exploring the wooded area behind the house with Herbie. I found some comfort exploring nature but still cried myself to sleep, thinking about my life and all that was left behind. Mom drove me into the city to finish out the remainder of the softball season but the following year, she refused to make the commute and my glory days of Little League were over. In my book, this was another nail in the coffin. My last hope of holding on to something of my own was gone and this was quite unsettling. We only saw Grandma and Grandpa over the holidays and I couldn't help but feel that I was a prisoner. My thoughts were consumed with running away but I didn't know how to get back to the city and, for the first time, considered killing myself. It seemed the only way to get out of here, away from Mario, away from everything.

School started and I remember my first day very clearly. Nobody wore uniforms the first few days and Mom wanted me to wear something nice and new. I had beat up most of my wardrobe, playing hard in my favorite jeans and T-shirts Grandma Zofie provided. I did have new clothes …oh yes …so new that the tags still hung from them. I buried them in the back of the closet for a reason. Have you seen the movie classic "A Christmas Story" when Ralphie gets a pink bunny pajama suit from a relative? The same relative that always buys him crazy clothes that he absolutely loathes? Against his plea, his mother insists he go put it on. As he came down the stairs his younger brother laughed hysterically and Ralphie was completely embarrassed and wanted to crawl in a hole. Luckily, his father understood and told him to take it off. Similarly, these are the clothes that Grandma Rita or "Sweetie" bought for me. And for that first day of school, that day of ever important first impressions, Mom dug out white dress pants that had huge ladybugs printed all over them from top to bottom. They were loud! Maybe they would've passed for preschool, but sixth grade? Of course, I put up a fight but didn't win. At least she didn't make me wear a dress. She learned that lesson very early on and I made all kinds of noise about that! There still lurked a light blue wraparound skirt with gray squirrels all over it, stashed in the furthest corner of the closet and she knew that if I only had two options, I would go for the pants.

After years of receiving such bizarre patterns, I earned my mother's sympathy, but those ladybugs! When I stepped into the new classroom, every eye stared at me and those pants. The tough girl strut carried me to my seat through the thick sea of judgement and I wanted to scream, "This is NOT who I am and if you keep staring at me, I'll SHOW you who I really am!" I'm certain my face reflected this as the teacher introduced me as the new student coming from the big city. Unease glazed over the room and all eyes went quickly to the floor. I said to myself, "Hmm . . . city girl. They're afraid of a city girl. I guess there won't be any trouble and I can relax." I don't know what I did with those pants when I got home, but I never wore them again.

I made friends with the boys first. They were always acting up and this was right up my alley. We shared the same sense of raw humor and I was not afraid to play rough or be disruptive in the middle of a lesson. Starting a spitball war or making rude noises while the teacher wrote on the chalk board became ritual. I discovered an uncanny ability to make my peers laugh and involve them in the frolic. The girls seemed too boring and they noticed how much fun me and the boys were having. I could tell that I intimidated them so it was time to break the ice.

I showed a couple of the girls sitting near me how to turn their Bic pen into a super-duper spitball blowgun machine. All you had to do was take out the ball point connected to the plastic ink holder and remove the round blue plug at the end of the pen and you're ready to go! The tapered end was the mouthpiece side used to load your ammo. Just tear off a small piece of paper and chew it until it's wet enough to form a ball. It took some practice to get the perfect sized spitball. Too large and it would plug the gun. Too small and it wouldn't fly very far and affected your aim. You also had to make sure it was wet enough so that it would stick to the target which was usually somebody's head. Slowly and carefully, you scan the room looking for a victim. It could be a friend that joined in retaliation before finding their own target, but the best was always an innocent bystander. These people would either get mad or better yet, not know what hit them as they brush their hand over their hair, thinking a bug flew at them. All was done under the radar which made the game exciting and challenging. Timing was key to not getting caught and you had to display incredible amounts of self-control because if you laughed out loud, you would be noticed. If you were caught however, you could gain respect and send chuckles to your friends by handling the situation bravely. Don't tell on your friends, say you're sorry for disrupting the class and try to keep a straight face. And so, the introductions were made, and I was now a part of the new school.

As weeks passed, things got a little easier. I still hated my living situation, but me and my new friend Sonny started hanging around after school. We frequented a local bowling alley and he was the first to visit my home. He was into computers long before they were easy to use. The Windows operating system had not been invented yet and everything was done in DOS. PC games were in their infancy, consisting of dots, dashes and bleeps as Pac Man arrived on the scene. Everything was stored on a 'floppy' disk which computers today don't even accommodate anymore. It all sounds like a prehistoric age and I still can't get over how fast the technology evolved.

Sonny had shown me some neat things on his computer but, because it could take over an hour to load a program, I never seemed to have a long enough attention span for it. He was completely fascinated with it and spent endless hours in his room on that old dinosaur learning its language. Nowadays, the world is reliant on these machines and Sonny's the man who can talk to them. No college education, just pure love that turned him into a sought-after computer programmer. Nice! While he was on his computer, I entertained myself by looking through his Dungeons & Dragons books. This fantasy world was cool and allowed me to use my imagination. I also stumbled upon some Tarot cards which REALLY interested me. I thought the artwork on each card was beautiful and they sparked a curiosity to learn more about them. I wondered if they could be helpful and offer clarity to my questions about my life.

The first person I met in Sonny's family was his mother, in a bit of an unusual fashion. Sonny, his friend and I entered the house and headed towards his room. Me and the guys were laughing and making jokes about sex. This was a usual topic for our young, perverted minds and I remembered exclaiming, "You don't know what an orgasm is?" Immediately, we heard a voice from the next room, "Sonny! Come here!"

He went to her and she asked who the slut was in the house. I was then asked to come in and introduce myself. I tossed my hair back and held my tough girl composure as I approached a petite redheaded woman sitting in a recliner, staring hard at me with her curious brown eyes. Sonny said, "This is Sylvia." I nodded my head at her and told her in a strong, proud voice that I was from the big city. She asked me what we were talking about in the other room and I responded by saying with even more surprise in my voice, "You don't know what an orgasm is EITHER?"

I think she gave me a little speech about how they didn't talk that way around the house and then she asked me if I played any sports. My spine straightened with dignity, "I'm a pitcher!" She informed me that she was the basketball coach for the school and suggested that I try out for the team. I followed her advice, for lack of something better to do, and made the cut. With more encouragement from her, track and volleyball followed shortly after. Sonny's two younger sisters, Raven and Rose, played sports too. Me and the girls bonded quickly and their baby brother, Jason, was a little cutie that seemed to like me. I realized that I was surrounded by a very supportive and fun family. I met their father, Mr. Bitar, and was a little intimidated at first, but I eventually warmed up to him as he came to some of our basketball games and rooted us on. This was something I wasn't used to and was elated as I experienced a closeness to these people.

My own family was …well …I wasn't sure. Trying to grow? But things were not as normal as everyone else seemed to enjoy. Home was miserable and I fled to my hideouts in the woods behind the house frequently. At least I had the Bitar family and another classmate came into my life.

Jane lived around the corner and, after school, I shared my secret hideout locations with her. As time went on, we grew close and I considered her my best friend. There were many sleepovers, mostly at her house, and though there were numerous differences in our tastes and background experiences, we complemented each other well. I was a tomboy/jock and she was a cheerleader/girly girl. She liked Barbie dolls and I was into Star Wars action figures. Her mother made her take dancing and piano lessons all while learning to be crafty in the 4H Club. I, on the other hand, was learning to be crafty in a whole different way. I made her laugh and feel a little dangerous as she made me feel important and funny. When I was around her or the Bitar family, I wanted to behave myself. Both were now the two most important entities of stability that were recognizable and they appeared at just the right time.

I really tried to like Mom's boyfriend. Now that I was making friends and settling into the new neighborhood, I lightened up, but there was still an anger towards him for taking us away from our old neighborhood. When he asked me if he and my mother could get married, I quickly snapped with another abrupt "NO!" Mario jokingly said, "Okay. I guess we can't." He looked at my mom, laughing. Both were laughing. I knew my opinion didn't matter so why bother asking me? Something wasn't right. In fact, it was terribly wrong, but what? I tried to work through these feelings and sometimes found myself laughing with them, but I couldn't shake the dark cloud and didn't understand why Mom wasn't seeing it. More frustration set in when Mom saw Jane's baby sister in a stroller and said, "I want one!" Mario heard this and replied, "Oh you do, ehh?" Shortly thereafter, I was driving in the car all dressed up and on our way to the Justice of the Peace to witness their marriage. I clearly remember the song by The Beatles on the radio as we headed there, "You Say Yes, I Say No". I thought I was the only one who heard the universe mocking me! As my head dizzied with fury, the best-man laughed out loud and repeated the lines to us in the car. He found the irony ridiculously funny and so did I. This whole thing had to be a bad dream.

I tried to be happy for my mother and played along, pretending to enjoy myself at the wedding reception in our basement. I even made a creative "Congratulations" sign to add to the decorations in an attempt to show I was going along with all of this. By the end of the night, or should I say early the next morning, I had a conversation with a drunken guest as I sipped on an alcoholic beverage to numb my head. I was not comforted by any words. The only thing I could do now was sleep because "There" was the only escape while I was "Here".

Two weeks after the wedding, the shadow of darkness that had consumed my thoughts and feelings showed its ugly face and confirmed my beliefs, proving my ...well ...let's just say ...astute observations. Mario and his friend were out drinking all day and when they finally stumbled into the house late, Mom was pissed. I went to my room and tried to stay out of the way when she asked Mario's friend to leave. There was a slight problem. He didn't drive. Mom thought that, rather than waiting for a cab, it would be quicker to get him out by offering to drive him. Mario didn't like this idea and that's when the argument broke out. He yelled at her. She yelled at him. The friend said it would be a good idea for him to go. Now the two pals were exchanging words. There is no arguing with a drunk, as all rationality goes completely out the window. I could feel the tension from my room as voices grew louder and obscenities filled the house. Mom grabbed her keys and insisted on taking the guy home! End of conversation! She wasn't gone long and upon her return she retreated to her bedroom across the hall from mine.

I sat on my floor playing with baseball cards, remaining silent behind my closed door. Mario walked into their bedroom, shut the door behind him, and began arguing with my mother. He called her a bitch and a fucking asshole in addition to other things that I couldn't hear clearly through the muffle of the doors. As the bickering continued, I suddenly heard Mom yelp at the top of her voice, as if she was struck. Next, there were the sounds of things being knocked over in the room. I opened my door a crack to hear the commotion better. A pause of silence. Was it over? And then, "You want some more, ehh?" It started up again and now I stood in the hallway staring at their door. His shouting scared me as the impact of his fists struck her over and over. Mom's distressed whimpers grew louder, and I quickly ran to the phone. Rather than calling 911, my first instinct was to call Grandma Zofie. With hands shaking, I quickly dialed, and the panic consumed me as the line kept ringing and no one was there. "No more time!" I rushed to the bedroom door again but didn't hear any screams or cries. Only gurgling, gagging, choking noises came through. I gathered up all my strength and flung the door open to find Mario's hands around her neck, squeezing her breath away. As soon as he saw me, he released his grip and hugged my mother, hiding what he had done to her face in his arm and said, "Aww …come here honey," trying to make it look like he was consoling her. I scanned the room and saw a large pool of blood in the middle of the bed and droplets of blood splattered on the walls, floor and light switch. This was the scene of a brutal beating. Five more seconds and it would have been the site of a murder had I not interrupted. I cried and screamed, "I'm calling Grandma!" I knew she wasn't home, but something compelled me to say it anyway and I ran out of the room. A soft, weak voice peeped from my mother. "No …don't do that." I ran to the rotary phone to let them hear me dialing. Mario slapped her a couple more times and then miraculously fled in his car.

Calling 911 was going to be my next move. Why I chose to announce "Grandma" is beyond me but it worked! My mind raged, and my heart dangled on a fine thread as Mom made her way to the bathroom. I walked into her bedroom and looked around again in disbelief. There was so much blood! It was everywhere! I went to find my mother sitting on the toilet seat with her head down. I grabbed a washcloth and cried as I tried to help clean up her face and arms. It was obvious she needed a hospital; her face looked like it was beaten with a baseball bat. My eleven-year-old voice said to her, "See? Now do you believe me? Will you leave him now?" The thread that my heart hung from snapped when she replied, "Sometimes people make mistakes." WTF! What was THAT supposed to mean? I was speechless, rattled and scared. "Where did he go?" How she knew, I don't know but replied, "His mother's house." We cleaned as much blood off her as we could and took a ride to his parent's place so they could see what he did. Sure enough, as we pulled up, his car was in the driveway. Mom told me to stay put. She thought I had seen enough and I obeyed her request. When she returned about a half-hour later, I asked how it went. Mom didn't say much, only that his parents were horrified and supportive of her.

My mother didn't go to the hospital until the following morning. She was treated for multiple injuries and her face was unrecognizable. Scared and embarrassed by what happened, she told the doctors she was mugged in a supermarket parking lot. She asked me not to tell anyone about the beating and to go along with her story. Of course, I was furious but obeyed her wishes and we lied about what happened for the next few months until her face restored itself.

That day, when she was at the hospital being treated, the monster came home, walked into the living room where I sat watching TV on the couch, and sat across the room to join me. I looked down and stewed in a violent silence, refusing to look at him. The hair stood on the back of my neck as I sensed his eyes staring at me, and my adrenaline rose to dangerous levels. He broke the silence; "I guess you're really mad at me, huh?" A sarcastic snicker came from the lump in my throat as gazed at the floor. His reply shocked me; "Do you mind telling me what happened?" My thoughts were, "You've got to be kidding me!" I turned my head and looked him straight in the eye. My blood boiled and I could feel the hate from deep within, now darting out of my eye sockets, wanting to rip out his heart and mutilate his face. He read this very well and asked me again to tell him; he didn't remember. My eyes turned away from this pathetic being to look at the floor again. In a low voice I began describing, with every last bit of patience I had, the gruesome details of the night before. When I got to the part about the strangulation, I heard sniffling and shifted my eyes to him. His hand was holding his head and he was sobbing like a baby. I stopped mid-sentence and glared at him. With doubt in my tone, "You don't remember any of this?" Now he cried harder and shook his head. For a second, I felt compassion and thought about what Mom said about people making mistakes. But this would be hard to set aside. Especially when I watched my mother feed herself through a straw because her jaw was so damaged, her lips were completely purple, and her teeth were loose. No, it was too early for forgiveness!

Mom wasn't leaving this guy and that meant I was stuck. Her decision was a huge disappointment to say the very least. She had made miscalculations in the past, but nothing compared to this. That was the day I lost respect for my mother and inner anger towards her was born. Why had I been forsaken? Every single time I had to lie for her was an added loss to her credibility as a responsible mother. Every year for the next five years there were always things to hide. After a while, it was hard to keep my mouth shut and, for my own sanity, I began writing. There were the normal daily drinking binges accompanied by name calling, camping trips gone bad, and times that mom would get a few slaps. I hoped she would come to her senses as the verbal abuse became directed towards me, but it didn't make a difference.

My brother was born a year after the strangulation and I remember the pregnancy. Mom seemed excited and tried to keep me involved by letting me know when the baby was kicking so I could place my hand on her belly. At first, I wasn't sure how I felt about it. Would giving this man a baby, straighten his ass out and calm him down? While she was pregnant, Mario was verbally abusive but didn't beat her so maybe this was going to be okay. I was getting used to being called a punk, piss pot, and "no good like your mother," amongst other insults that were quite nasty. We completely rejected each other and I gave him absolutely NO respect (something he always demanded) and he never understood why. This angered him because his ego was so inflated. It was as if he was some sort of prize that we were not worthy of. Oh please! Respect is earned and he had the wrong idea of how to earn it.

When my brother was born, I saw a glimmer of hope. Mario was in the delivery room for the birth and was the first to hold him. He was utterly blown away by the experience and seemed to be a proud father, handing out cigars to everyone and celebrating with his Old Vienna beer, of course. Mom looked worn out when she arrived home but had a gleam in her eyes.

A son. A beautiful son. And he WAS beautiful! The cutest baby I have ever seen! I fell in love immediately and remember being nervous when I held him the first few times. I loved cradling him in my arm and watching his big blue eyes stare back at me while I gave him his bottle. It was fun to watch him eat as his tiny nose breathed strongly and he gulped down the milk, making little grunts and moans of approval. His head was soft and it smelled good. His facial expressions were hysterical, especially when he was pooping. I was good at making him smile and laugh out loud and this was a positive change to the daily routine. Even though Mario was up to his old habits, like losing his license to DWI, the focus for Mom was the baby. I helped as he grew …bathing, spoon feeding, changing diapers, playing, watching and walking him in the stroller. I entertained him and though he didn't know it, he entertained me too, and as we formed a bond, I developed a love and care for him that was very protective. His hurt was mine and I would always try to protect him from harm if I could.

About eight months passed and the atmosphere was more relaxed, though I never completely let my guard down. One day, Mario went out on foot to have a few drinks. Hours later, my mother found him at the local bar and asked if he could please come home. He argued with her in front of the bar patrons. As everyone stared, the debate moved outside where he then grabbed her and started pulling the hair out of her head. Clumps of it lay inside her car, on the ground and in his hand as she broke away from him, ripping her shirt. She went back into the bar and asked everyone to call the police but they didn't want to get involved. Mom left and made the call herself as soon as she got home. When I saw her ripped shirt and bald patches, I cried as the horrific bullshit returned. Luckily, as Mario approached the house, the cops pulled up. He tried to hide under the front bushes, but they found him with their flashlights. They were both questioned and then police took Mario away. I was relieved, until they released him in the middle of the night when his buzz wore off, and we were awoken by a pounding on the back door accompanied by shouts to let him in, just like the big bad wolf. I don't recall opening the door and don't think we did, but I'm sure there are things that I've blocked out. What I do remember is that there was so much hair missing from my mother's head that she couldn't walk around in public. She snuck over to a local hair dresser for a cut and perm as an attempt to cover the bald spots until it grew back in.

Of course, the lies were in place. Grandma Zofie had dinner on every major holiday and Mario never came to the gathering. The first time was enough. He didn't care for my mother's family, especially her brother, which was fine with me! I looked forward to these special occasions and didn't want him to ruin it. But this year, even in his absence, he did. Everyone noticed the front of Mom's head and somebody asked her about it at the dinner table. I wanted to stand up and exclaim the truth about everything that had been going on these past few years. I wanted my family to come to the rescue and get us out. As I pondered this wonderful thought, ready to speak, Mom spoke up and gave this 'way out there' lie about her hair naturally falling out and that she was going to be tested for cancer. WTF! The whole table just stared at her in horror and concern. I knew my uncle was skeptical, but the issue was dropped and we finished our dinner. My eyes sunk into my plate and I tried to enjoy this delicious Thanksgiving food, but was weighed down by the heartbreak and disappointment my mother was putting me through. The heat burned in my chest and the defeat numbed my senses.

My thoughts were sidetracked for a while after dinner and I gave thanks for this small blessing. It was the time when my first cousins and I went down into the basement to play. I loved it down there! This was where Grandpa Loosha's darkroom was, along with his office, workshop and bar area. Now that the days of driving out to the farm every weekend with my grandparents were gone, these brief holiday visits with my cousins were sacred. It was always a somber moment for me when they had to leave, "If only they knew where I had to go." Misery and despair were now my home and there was no way out.

I found myself going to the Bitar's house on an almost daily basis. Learning to play basketball enabled me to burn off some steam which proved to be healthy. I took a real shine to Mrs. Bitar and developed friendships with other kids on the team, including Addy and her brother Zak. Turns out, they had a highly dysfunctional family as well and we bonded instantly. Our twisted sense of humor totally connected us in a way that only people experiencing mental abuse and alcoholism can understand. To most, it wouldn't seem funny to joke about how the Christmas tree was purposely knocked over or hearing from your loved one, "You have nothing to be proud of!" The laugher we shared was a healing salve on an open wound. Addy and Zak were truly a blessing!

Mrs. Bitar was a gift. As a coach, she taught me discipline and by her words and actions, she earned my love and respect. Her passion for the game was inspiring and she made me feel important as a player. Off the court, she was caring, funny, and possessed an uncanny ability to read me extremely well. Setting aside the terrible first impression I had shown the day I met her, she opened her heart and home to me. Though I was friends with all of her children, most of my visits to the house were to see her. As Sonny put it to me many years later, "You know how Mom is with stray animals!" I was definitely a stray that kept hanging around and was finally adopted. I found safety there and was especially fascinated with the family dynamics of a mother and father with four kids. They were so entertaining! And besides a few minor squabbles, everyone got along! Respect, no violence, no name calling. This was a foreign and enchanting habitat.

Mr. Bitar was mysterious to me in those days. He worked a lot and everyone tiptoed around him not wanting to make him mad. I wasn't sure how to take this, but I noticed how supportive and involved he was when he could be. He allowed us kids to come in and out of his home which was CONSTANT as we always dropped by unannounced. It was like there was some sort of magnetic field surrounding the place and we were drawn there like a moth to a flame.

Mrs. Bitar was good at extracting information from me. She always knew when something was wrong and made me feel comfortable enough to share my thoughts. Finally! Someone to talk to …someone I could trust. Someone I could look up to …someone that cared enough to listen. I started calling her "Ma" and she was exactly that to me. I spent many nights sobbing on her couch as she wrapped her arms around me with a love so great, she could only have come from heaven. Words cannot express my gratitude!

In the meantime, my depressing family bought a three-story house, making more room for us to spread out. I liked it. My brother and I each had our own rooms, but I immediately gravitated to the attic and spent most of my time there. I took it upon myself to staple cardboard up onto the slanted roof studs and hung a curtain to form a wall, making what looked like a studio apartment to create a little sanctuary for myself. I took my stereo up there with an old couch, coffee table and beanbag chair to chill out and enjoy peace and quiet. I hung up concert posters, started writing poetry, and played my acoustic guitar that I bought after winning a jackpot at Bingo with Grandma Zofie. Mario took notice of this and made an attempt to be nice by letting me use his Gibson electric guitar and amplifier. He scored big points there and I spent many hours jamming and letting the music take me away.

Mario and I tried to get along and make the best of things, but he kept blowing it. He ruined my eighth-grade graduation party with his drunken rudeness which made the guests uncomfortable. My mother seemed a million miles away and all I did was stew in my anger. I daydreamed about how to get back at Mario. I wanted to kill him but that seemed unrealistic. I wasn't going to waste my life going to jail for him …he had taken enough from me as it was. With hours of contemplation, I figured it out. I knew how to hurt him. I would take away from him what he prized most. Money! He had wads of it lying around! I grew bold and took his money as often as possible, snatching a couple of hundred-dollar bills at a time, every few days.

Mario was also a pot dealer and by that time, I was smoking on occasion. One of the girls from the basketball team got me high and I liked how it made me feel for the most part. I finally understood why Mom and her friends indulged themselves when I was little. This new-found hobby of mine was to be supplied by Mario's huge stash. There were pounds and pounds of it bagged up in the basement and I helped myself as often as possible. At first, he blamed Mom for stealing his money and dope. I heard the arguments numerous times as she denied any knowledge, but by now, I didn't feel bad that she might take a beating for it. She got us into this situation and knowingly allowed it to continue, so maybe this was a little payback for her as well. I had now officially entered my rebellious teenage years! When Mom questioned me about Mario's stuff …denial. He never accused me, but tried to be smart and put a padlock on the door in the basement. I would find the key and get in. When he started carrying the key, I carefully removed the hinges on the door every time I wanted to get in. I was determined to fuck with him and had plenty of time to do it. "Aahh!" A sigh of justice!

It was an insane time for me and I don't know if my mother was mindful of the negative direction I was heading towards. She gave me something though, and it took me by surprise. One evening, she came to my room and delivered a letter that my father wrote to me when I was a baby. I couldn't believe it! I held the yellow lined paper in my pulsating hands like an ancient sacred script, and read it carefully, numerous times. It said:

To my little one,

I hope that by the time you are able to read this, the earth will have transcended to where education is no longer boring and unattractive, we love and understand people from all parts, and life becomes beautiful once more and not a menace as it is now. I know, myself and others are trying to rebuild a beautiful world from the poor thing my parents and their friends left me. I hope you will follow, and if you succeed then we might have everlasting peace. Above all, you must straighten out your head and the heads of others before physical things can begin to be accomplished.

Reading this letter was the spark that ignited my deep interest in meditation, spiritualism, healing, and helping people. I wanted to follow his words and find the path to enlightenment. At that time, I had no direction but hoped that I would someday fulfill his wishes.

CHAPTER 5

BRANCHING OUT

THERE WERE NO MORE school sports to occupy my time. When I entered high school, I was immediately turned off by the 'clicky' people. This new group of jocks was not my style and I kept myself separated. Jane and I had a long talk with each other just before entering this new phase of our lives. It was obvious that she was going to be the high energy cheerleading type and I was going to be the smoking, jean jacket, concert T-shirt wearing troublemaker. These two groups did not mesh well in high-school and we made a promise that, no matter what, we would be friends. And we kept that promise! It was more like the "odd couple" from an outsider's point of view. We seemed so dissimilar and had opposite backgrounds, yet we understood one another. Jane was privy to all of what was really going on at my house and empathized. She had a full understanding of why I did the things I did and never judged me for it. She was more frightened for me than anything else when she saw the company I was keeping. The guy I lost my virginity to at the tender age of fourteen was really bad news and so were his friends. Jane knew I was in for some grief.

Deep down I was depressed, but partying with my friends and getting a lot of sexual attention from men in their twenties kept my mind occupied and gave me a sense of purpose. These guys turned me on to LSD and I escaped reality with a couple of close girlfriends on a regular basis. I just wanted to have fun, feel joy in my life, and escape the burdens I carried on my shoulders, even if it was temporary. I was a young girl craving much needed love and attention and didn't know any better. I agreed to do anything for my boyfriend, thinking he loved me, but I didn't agree when he brought his buddies into the room. They were always checking me out, making passes at me, and I wondered why my boyfriend seemed unaffected. All of them were in their early twenties, knowingly drugging and taking advantage of a naïve minor and had I known better, I would've had them jailed. Everything I was told was a lie and I found out what it meant to be used. There were other guys I dated that were an improvement, but I never seemed happy with them.

Hanging out with my girls was the healthier thing to do. We partied, went to concerts, hung out and supported each other through those awkward teenage blues. We got high every morning on the corner across the street from the school before heading into ninth-grade homeroom and celebrated the end of the school day by smoking some more. My supply of weed was endless. 'Ma' Bitar was very perceptive, worried, and had a bad feeling about something and told me to be careful. I thought I had everything under control and told her not to worry. For once, I was actually feeling pretty good. A couple months later, I was sitting in eighth-period science class with Jane, watching the clock, anticipating the end of the day when the phone rang and the teacher answered it. He looked at me and said, "Yes... OK. Yes... Ok," and hung up the phone. I had no idea what was going on as the vice principal appeared and instructed me to take him to my locker. Now, as we walked down the hall, I broke into a sweat and felt the butterflies in my belly. When I opened my locker, he went through everything and found my mom's pipe in my jacket pocket. "Oh no!" I thought, "I'm so busted!" Earlier that morning I had stolen a big bag of weed from Mom's jacket hanging in the closet. Now I was handing it over to the school. F*&#K!! First, they called the police and then my mother, before questioning me. They wanted to know where I got everything and said they had been watching me and my friends from the window getting high on the corner for quite some time. Wasn't this a bitch! Now I was scared. What will I do? What should I say? The only thing I could think of was my baby brother. If the cops knew about the tons of dope in our house that supplied me, they would also find out about Mario's abusive behavior and most certainly take my brother away. I was terrified! With that thought, I lied and said I found everything in a nearby junkyard. Of course, they didn't believe me, but I stuck to the story and they couldn't move forward. I was suspended from school for a week and Mom came to pick me up. She barked at me, asking where I got the pot and the pipe, knowing it was hers. When I snapped back and said it WAS hers and I didn't tattle, a dead silence overcame her.

Court put me on probation and, like a dumb ass, I got busted in school again two months later for passing a note with the price for the speed I was selling. They never found anything but a bunch of single dollar bills crinkled up in my pocket from fast hallway sales. The cheerleaders and jocks loved the stuff and I was able to get it for them upon request from one of the twenty-year-old dudes I was hanging with. He told me the pills were quite legal, ordered out of a catalog he showed me, but I guess you can't distribute them at school! Now I was suspended for a month and placed under house arrest. I was given more probation and mandatory drug counseling after being threatened to spend time in a juvenile facility. Little did they know that being under house arrest was probably the worst punishment in my case, but I was so scared, I was happy with the sentencing!

Counseling seemed like a joke to me. Maybe it works for some troubled teens, and I certainly encourage it, but people forget what their own minds were like as a teenager. Parents, the system, whomever, assume that professional help will have quick and positive results. POOF! All is well. Everything is better. In my case, I put on a good front because the law was watching but I was a mess on the inside. All I could focus on in that counseling room was that huge tumor, bump, boil or whatever it was positioned smack dab in the middle of his forehead. There was no way I could pay attention to anything else! Now, mind you I was a teenager. As he spoke, I thought, "Does he realize how nasty that thing looks? How did it get there? I wonder if he's tried to pop it." Then I realized he asked me a question.

"Hmm. Yes. No. I don't know."

I told him whatever he wanted to hear just so I could get the hell out of there. I dreaded the boredom and wondered, on every car ride to see him, if the thing on his forehead went away yet. I don't recall how many times I had to sit with him but remember the relief when it was over.

Jane was the only friend I was allowed to see. She brought my homework to the house and if it wasn't for her, I would have failed the ninth grade. Cell phones didn't exist yet so it was tough to communicate and I would sneak to make quick calls to my friends from the house phone. I really missed going to the Bitar's to escape my fears and troubles. Being stuck in that house watching Mario drink his usual case of beer sucked! I could tell when he went into oblivion as he started talking to himself. This creeped me out and I remember calling Ma Bitar a couple times, crying and scared. Her anger over the situation lent me some mental support.

My mother wasn't home much anymore. She was making an effort to get herself a job in real estate that a new friend got her into. She was excited about it; to go back to school and learn something new. Once she received her license, she could start making her own money. In her absence, I watched my brother quite a bit, especially during my suspension from school. I learned a hard lesson that year and decided to steer clear of the law. There was no way I was giving up a couple of my party friends; they were much more than that, but I completely dissolved any relations I had with the "bad boys" and cut way down on the drug usage through the tenth and eleventh grade.

By my junior year, I unknowingly developed the reputation of being the "toughest girl in school", as someone put it to me later on. I got into a fight with a senior and put up a good show but lost with a black eye. My attitude and ambition for a rematch after my eye healed earned me a big pair of brass balls which apparently scared the girl off. I found myself defending Jane a lot and took on an entire group of people for her over something stupid. This clique gave her a real hard time, accusing her of stealing a boyfriend. I got a couple of my buddies involved and we harassed these jerks until they apologized and left Jane alone. I was glad to finally do something positive with this bad reputation. Although I had enemies, they stayed away from me and that was good.

I made new friends that liked to skip class as much as me. I did my homework and actually improved my grades but had the need to do what "I wanted" on occasion. In the adult working world, we call it a mental health day; an absolute necessity! I had a few new boyfriends here and there, trying to find that 'special someone' but love eluded me. I experienced a certain loneliness and separateness that I couldn't explain, so I spoke to God on occasion asking, "Why, why, why?" There were a few parents that didn't care for me hanging around with their kids. On the outside, I knew it didn't look good because of the whole drug bust thing a couple years prior. I was labeled and no matter how hard I tried to stay off drugs and behave, the stigma followed me. I still wore my comfortable jean jacket and T-shirts which made me look like a hoodlum. But inside . . . I knew I wasn't. I felt extremely misunderstood. Deep down, I was sensitive and had a lot of love to give. I had wisdom to share if someone would just listen. My intentions were good and I wanted to have meaningful relationships with people that loved me for ME.

One day, in my junior year, while walking down the crowded hallway to class, this tall, long haired brunette wearing a Doors T-shirt caught my attention. Our paths crossed frequently and I noticed her going into my friend's typing class. I couldn't explain it, but there was this overwhelming draw that told me I had to meet her. The lingering sensation was like nothing I had encountered before as our eyes met for a split second and then on we went. I asked my friend about this mysterious person and she told me the girl was weird, so I laughed it off and made attempts to forget about it. One day, I went to the lunch room and as I looked for a place to sit, I heard my name called. A friend was waving for me to come and play a card game called Euchre. They were short one player and Jess, the "mystery girl", needed a partner. I walked over, sat down across from her, and we started the game. When our eyes met, we both smiled as if we'd known each other forever, and a spark ignited. My heart and senses were given life as if I'd been brought back from the dead.

Jess and I started hanging out after school and I met some of her friends, including her boyfriend. When I met her family, only her grandmother seemed to like me, but I was used to that sort of thing. One evening, we were at her boyfriend's apartment sitting on the couch watching TV. He had a cute little puppy that jumped up and lay between us and as we both petted him, our hands touched. Another spark! We sat quietly, nervous and excited, as we explored each other's hand, tracing the lines and curves until her boyfriend walked in the room. Our hands quickly pulled away and the moment was over.

In school, Jess and I constantly passed notes to each other, mostly discussing and analyzing this new and strange magnetism that consumed our thoughts night and day. We tried to be around each other as much as possible and had an occasional sleepover at my house. I looked forward to this because her boyfriend wasn't around to be a menace. Nothing else in the world existed when I was with her. What was all this? It wasn't until we were alone on her grandmother's couch talking one night that we really figured it out. We sat close, holding hands. I remember being so nervous I was sweating and thought I was going to black out. With attempts to keep my cool as my heart furiously pounded in my chest, I noticed that hers was doing the same and I wondered if this was TRUE love. The intense energy in the depths of my soul convinced me that it was. Gazing deeply and getting lost in each other's eyes, the irresistibility drew us in for our first kiss. It was absolutely unparalleled and no one had ever given me the chills like that. Now I knew the meaning of seeing fireworks! I was finally home! Shortly after, consumed in love, we consummated the relationship. I would love to describe the details, but it's not that kind of book!

But wait! Wasn't this something you were supposed to feel with a man? Confusion set in for both of us, especially her. We talked about it and agreed that no one could find out. In 1986, being gay in high school in a small town was not an okay thing to be or even experiment with. We'd lose all our friends, get a bad reputation, and be a source of mockery. I remember in ninth grade, there was a rumor started about a girl in swimming class who supposedly looked at other girls while changing in the locker room. Since that day, and for the remainder of high school, she was made fun of and avoided like the plague. I don't even think the rumor was true, but watching what that poor girl endured was enough to be 'straight' at all costs. All the wonderful feelings that Jess and I finally discovered had to be kept top secret. Every beautiful love letter we wrote to one another had to be destroyed. Her mother was starting to suspect that we were becoming intimate …or at least that I wanted to be intimate with her daughter. Jess kept her boyfriend around for cover. I always wished she would have dumped him for me but I understand why she didn't. It was painful to share her and this sparked jealously and tormenting mental anguish. When she told me she would cry, thinking of me as they had sex, it brought comfort to know that she only wanted me, but the thought of them together was something I couldn't bear and didn't want to hear.

All the beautiful words Jess expressed, and all the intense emotion filled me up and kept me hanging on. A few months into our relationship, unbeknownst to me, her boyfriend found a love note in her back pocket that was very telling. Jess panicked, told a bunch of lies, and very abruptly cut all ties with me, giving no explanation. I was totally dumbfounded! I didn't know if I had done something wrong and so, my world was crushed in a matter of seconds as she refused to see or talk to me. All I wanted was an explanation, but I didn't get one.

Never in my life had I experienced something more painful. This far surpassed any mental cruelty I'd been exposed to at home. I withdrew into myself that summer and considered suicide again, but this time it was very serious. All this gay stuff had to be kept quiet. It was so taboo and the fear choked me so much that I couldn't even share it with Ma Bitar. Even when she knew I was in a bad way and wanted to know what was going on, I remained silent. I am thankful that, even though she didn't understand, she stood by me anyways with her love and support. My entire senior year was consumed with major depression. All year long I had to walk passed Jess and say nothing. Just looking at her took my breath away and my heart was in shreds. The unbearable heaviness would have sunk me to the bottom of the sea, if I had jumped. It took years to recover from this. My friends noticed the melancholy and assumed it was related to my family. But at the house, things were finally starting to change.

My mother discovered some of Mario's secrets that finally convinced her to leave him. To put it in a nutshell, he was paying prostitutes from out of town and having phone sex for masturbation purposes while he was supposed to be watching his son. FINALLY! We were going to be free of him! He was ordered to leave the house and that changed everything for me. No more being grounded for a full month for being just one minute late. No more arguments and uncomfortable tension. The weight was lifted! Things were tough for Mom . . . for us . . . but we would get through it, just like old times. In the midst of my heartbreak over Jess, the changes in the house delivered happy feelings again, without the influence of drugs. And we had my brother! It would be hard for him to understand what was going on. He was only four or five at the height of the divorce and visiting with dad on the weekends proved confusing to him. Mom and Mario had a bitter separation and both used my brother as a tool to get back at one another. It sucks that kids suffer for their parents' immaturity. I could only hope my brother would grow up to understand this and escape the grips of a poisoned mind. I kept my fingers crossed for him.

The peace in the house was priceless and I did everything I could to help take care of my brother. I spent a lot of time babysitting, feeding and entertaining him while Mom worked. It was a new beginning but not the kind I expected. Out of spite, Mario didn't pay the child support and we couldn't afford the upkeep, so the house was lost. Mom's job went down the tubes and we were forced to go back on welfare. She tried holding down other jobs, mostly cleaning, but she'd had back surgery which limited her abilities and she ended up on permanent disability. It was then that I noticed a change in her. I couldn't pinpoint it at the time, but now realize that she felt defeated. Mom completely forgot about my sixteenth birthday and felt bad about it later. She was overwhelmed as we moved to an apartment and she buried her pain in a bottle, becoming an alcoholic. Suddenly, she was wasted all the time and failed to understand why I was so hurt and angered. After all we'd been through! This was the icing on the cake. My hope for her was gone.

Now that she was home all the time, I didn't babysit and made myself absent as much as possible. I was struggling with my own personal hang-ups, trying to graduate high school, and I just didn't have the energy to deal with her self-made problems. I felt bad for my brother, but there was nothing I could do. Mom loved him very much and all I wanted was for her to set a better example for him than she did with me. So far, that didn't seem likely. And then it dawned on me to turn this negative into a positive. "Wait! Mom gave me the BEST examples! I will do everything in my power NOT to be like her! I will not be an alcoholic or dope head. I will not live my life on welfare. I will definitely not allow anyone to hit me or disrespect me in any way, shape or form." I had the stubbornness and motivation to follow through on these self-promises. In retrospect, my mother was one of the best teachers of all!

When I graduated from high school, Mom was so happy. She always wished for me to be a success in whatever I chose and prayed that I didn't make the same mistakes she did. Not finishing high school was one of them, and as I walked across the stage to receive my diploma, she cried. As annoyed as I was with her, there remained a part of me that wanted to make her proud. This was a good day.

This summer was also the beginning of my independence. Many kids stay home for as long as they can to plan for college or to work and save money. I had no intention of furthering my education and wanted out as soon as possible. Mom decided to move back to the big city and, for all those years I wanted to return "home", I wasn't ready. I held down a summer job for the three previous years at a youth center which enabled me to utilize some of my creative talents. I had friends here, felt somewhat established, and couldn't bear the thought of leaving my family . . . the Bitar's. Living with my alcoholic mother was not an option. I had to do something . . . find somewhere to go. I considered my six-year old brother and hoped he wouldn't feel abandoned if I left.

I had a chat with a high school acquaintance and to my surprise, her mom was willing to rent me an extra bedroom for a hundred bucks a month. I moved in right away with my stereo, guitars, clothes and concert posters. I wrote my own songs and poems, and shared them with the youngest of the family; my new fourteen-year old housemate. We bonded immediately and she enjoyed hanging out in my room, laughing, and playing pranks on her bitchy, older sister. It was a blast!

Music and writing carried me through so much! I re-read the private notebook of poems I had written during the dark step-father days and it was such a relief to be free of that time in my life and even more amazing that I had gotten through it. Flipping through page after page of trials and tribulations, I came across a song I wrote about Mario and his drinking. It had won me second place in my tenth-grade talent show and I wondered if the rest of the material in my notebook would be useful someday.

Perhaps another song? An album? This idea lit my passion for music on fire and all I wanted to do was play. I was fortunate to have these outlets as a healthy distraction.

High school was now forever over and the freedom was refreshing! Removing myself from 'home' was even more rewarding! The independence was intoxicating. Of course, there were new stresses to discover in the adult world like paying rent, buying my own food and personal supplies. It wasn't as easy as I thought. My summer job was coming to an end and I needed to find work to maintain the ability to stay out on my own. Having extra cash to spend on myself for fun was hard to come by. I had a number of different jobs, exploring what I might like for long term. This was challenging for me. My dream was to be a rock star or famous writer, utilizing my gifts of creativity to help bring some awesomeness and healing into the world. When I realized there was no money to be made, at least not enough to keep me from going back home, I did what most creative people are forced to do. I settled for something unsuitable. At least I paid my rent on time.

After a year of living with my friend's family, circumstances changed, and I had to move on. Tension had been slowly building because I kept defending 'little sister' against 'bitchy sister'. The situation came to a head when we got into a scuffle in the living room. I was on the telephone with an important call and, out of nowhere, she came at me. I told the person on the line to hang on and quickly dropped the phone to defend myself. I rose out of the chair to direct my attention to the charging bull and plowed into her. She flew across the room onto the couch as I noticed 'little sister' and her friend at the top of the stairway watching and rooting me on to kick her ass. My opponent furiously kicked her legs up in the air to block my advances and managed to free herself from the couch. As we wrestled, my fist rose to punch her in the face and her mom walked in. I gently lowered my arm and said, "Oh Hi."

Yes, it was time to move on. Panic formed a bead of sweat on my brow. This was my first eviction of sorts and I just couldn't go back home. Fortunately, Ma Bitar came to the rescue and let me stay with them. "Dad" Bitar, as I was now calling him, was happy to accept extra money and help around the house. All four kids were still at home so there wasn't much space, but Rose shared her room with me. I was very thankful! Many positive things happened to me while I was there, and our bonds grew stronger as I was welcomed and made to feel like a part of the family. I admired and loved them so much! I decided to stop smoking weed and went back to school for art. "Dad" was a softball coach and talked me into playing softball again for his team and I discovered that I still had a great arm and maintained my home-run hitting skills. I was just now, at nineteen, experiencing my best years of softball. I had forgotten how much I loved the game and how cocky of a player I was when I first met "Ma".

I continued to date guys, though I was never happy. There were a couple men who were nice and treated me well, unlike the losers I started with, but the feelings of passion were always absent. I thought of Jess often and wondered what she was doing these days. I longed for closure. I'd made one more attempt at dating an older guy. He was really into me, taking me places, buying me things, and turned me on to the strategy of betting the ponies at the track. We got along well, and he was entertaining. We joked about how I was this nice young trophy on his arm. I wasn't in love, just going through the motions of living a straight life. He did turn me on to one thing that I grew to love and that was cocaine. I tried it in the past, but it was so expensive. I couldn't afford that type of high. This guy was a dealer and it was always available, free of charge. I had given up all the other drugs by now and only smoked cigarettes and drank socially here and there. Doing a little coke seemed harmless. I soon discovered that smoking it was even better. I had no idea what it was all about until he pulled out a glass pipe and cooked some up. Wow! What a rush! My addictive personality could get used to this. I looked at it as just experimenting.

In the meantime, Ma had some bad news and seemed very upset when she approached me. After a year of sharing a room with Rose, she wanted her room back. I knew what this meant. I could tell from the dismay on Ma's face that she was torn by the decision, but this was her daughter. I got too comfortable and forgot about the sacrifice Rose had made for me. I understood I couldn't stay there forever. I knew I couldn't afford a place by myself and the rest of my friends were either still at home or off to college. I definitely didn't want to live with the boyfriend and wouldn't consider it. Moving back with my mother was the only option. At least I would be closer to the art school and be able to see my brother more.

Mom had a second-floor apartment right on the edge of the little league field where I first played ball and Grandma and Grandpa were right around the corner. I finally made it back! Mom and I had some catching up to do and we had a few good belly laughs. I was making her proud again by furthering my education and sometimes she watched me work on a painting for school on the drawing table that Grandpa Loosha gave me. He supported anything I tried. He paid for my first year of guitar lessons years earlier and bought my first electric guitar amp. What a guy! I appreciated him so much and having his support and encouragement was priceless!

Sitting at the dinner table again with my brother was nice. He was eight years old now and the shock of time quickly passing by gave me a shiver. Mom said he looked up to me and that made me happy. If I had any bad habits left, and there were a few, I tried not to show it to him. This became a bit of a challenge though. My mother's alcoholism didn't disappear within those couple of years in my absence. Soon after moving home I realized that she and I had turned into oil and water. I was right back in the same old situation and it seemed I was stuck here for a while. We argued constantly about her rude drunkenness and that she was an embarrassment. Trying to set a curfew for me didn't sit well, after being out on my own for a couple years, so things became incredibly miserable in a hurry. Like before, I stayed away as much as I could.

I spent a lot of time at the boyfriend's house and fell into a downward spiral with cocaine. I became addicted and found myself hanging out only for the drugs and a place to escape my mother. It got so bad! I was smoking it all night long and snorting it at school during the day to stay awake. My art school friend partied with me, but noticed how excessive I was becoming. One night after he went to work, I continued smoking through the morning hours and nearly overdosed. "Just one more hit." My heart raced frantically, I broke into an instant sweat and my vision started to black out. The only thing I could think was, "What are they gonna say when they find out I died of a cocaine overdose? My God! I'm going to die like my father." I was burning up and gasping for air as my chest felt like it was about to explode. I didn't know why, but I stumbled and felt my way along the hallway walls to the back door, almost being pulled there. I ripped my shirt off and threw myself into the snow bank, trying to bring my body temperature down. I can't imagine what that looked like.

Somebody was watching over me that morning because the cold calmed me down and my vision returned. I went back in the house, sobered up, and left. I didn't tell the boyfriend what happened; just that things weren't working out and I ended the relationship.

I sweated out the cravings alone and it was agonizing, but I beat it. I was so depressed about my living situation and thoroughly disgusted with myself over the drug/boyfriend thing. I purchased my first car with student loan money after Grandma Rita refused to help, and focused on finishing art school. I needed to get a job and get out of that house. My mother and I knew it wasn't working out. One of her long-time friends owned a bar across the street and she asked him if he could hook me up. I really liked this guy. When I was much younger we visited him and he let me play his drum set. He knew my dad and thought of me as a daughter, so he started me off as a dishwasher, part-time. It was better than nothing.

As time went on, Mom became more and more irate as she drank and living with her was intolerable. I barely made any money and felt trapped once again. Suicidal thoughts revisited me, and I knew I'd better hurry up and do something, though there didn't seem to be any hope in sight. Completely defeated, I paced the kitchen and in the background, I overheard a conversation in the other room on the TV. Shirley MacLaine was on Oprah (I think) and was discussing how to align your "chakras". For some reason, I was drawn to the couch and took notes during the show on the colors of the rainbow that represented these "energy centers" in the body. I tried the suggested meditation that night and, to my surprise, I woke up feeling better than I ever had. (It wasn't until later in life that I discovered this to be called Reiki). A certain peace washed over me, and I suddenly had hope. The relief I experienced seemed like a miracle and I was reminded of an old curiosity about spirituality. This led to further exploration, through books, on the practice of meditation and connecting to our divine source.

At first, I had no idea of what to do and worried if what I was doing was being done correctly. Many books had different ideas and techniques to achieve a sense of peace and balance. My Catholic education encouraged prayer. I did pray, but discovered that by talking to God in my own heart-felt words, rather than the recitation of someone else's prayers, resulted in a stronger feeling of closeness to my maker. Getting hung up on the

RIGHT "how to's" proved to be a huge distraction. There are no wrong ways when it comes to meditating, but without this awareness, I set aside my efforts many times. Though I felt defeated and didn't think I could concentrate long enough for meditation, I still noticed an inner urgency to return to and connect with SOURCE. I decided to wing it and just go with whatever brought on a sense of comfort and peace within myself. Sometimes, it was just playing a musical instrument. Other times, I tried to look in the mirror and say nice things to myself, even if I didn't believe it yet. Eventually, I discovered that repeating these affirmations broke a barrier in my mind. This persistence produced an assumption that all was well, rather than the usual doom and gloom, and opened the door to allowing happier outcomes. Most times, I just laid in bed listening to my breath, in attempts to quiet my busy mind. This was MOST frustrating, but with practice it got easier.

With my new-found strength and motivation, I walked across the street and had a long talk with my boss explaining my problems and he was empathetic. There was a vacant apartment behind the bar. It was a hole in the wall but he offered to let me have it for one hundred bucks a month plus utilities. I thanked him and quickly accepted. He increased my hours at the bar as well, knowing that what he was paying me was going right back to him in rent. Things were getting brighter.

When Mom found out that her friend hooked me up with a place to live, she realized he was doing me a huge favor. She lightened up and became more tolerable. She and her boyfriend helped me clean the apartment and gave me an old kitchen table and some dishes. Grandma Zofie bought me silverware and gave me some towels and an old carpet. The Bitar's gave me their old couch after hearing that I only had a beanbag chair in the living room. I garbage picked my first coffee table and used cinder blocks and boards to proudly build a book shelf. Again, I felt blessed and thankful.

It was awesome to have a place all to myself! I found solace there and knew there was no choice but to work extremely hard to maintain a roof over my head. When winter hit, I learned just how high a gas bill could get. That was a real eye-opener. Between the bills for the apartment, food and transportation, the stress of not being able to keep my head above water led to taking on a roommate. Luckily, a friend was looking to get out of her house too and she gladly accepted the offer to split the bills. My security was reassured.

That year was very enlightening. I had taken control of my living situation and removed myself from negativity. I continued to study about meditation, prayer, and began paying more attention to the voice within. I wanted these things to be a permanent part of my life, offering balance. I always felt a sense of inner power throughout my life and, many times, I could feel vibrations in my hands that I didn't understand. It made me think of my father on the other side, wondering what it was like there, and imagining what he was learning.

I came out of the closet that year. It was one of the scariest and most stressful situations I'd ever encountered. At first, I didn't know who to tell. I found happiness in knowing my true self but was afraid that I'd lose friends and family over being gay. Most people, in the beginning, found out through the grapevine. When I was seen around town hanging out with a well-known lesbian, outside of the softball field, people talked. Of course, hanging out with someone who's gay shouldn't matter, but in my case, the rumors were true. Ma Bitar was shocked and hurt at first … more because I hadn't said anything. When I explained that I was afraid of losing her, she understood, although she was concerned that this would make my life even harder. I explained that these inner feelings were not a choice. They had been there all my life and I couldn't live a lie anymore; pretending to enjoy relationships with men and playing along, all for the approval of others. Now THAT made my life hard. My confusion and self-esteem issues cleared and I was no longer chained to the illusion of thinking that a man was necessary. Ma and the entire family supported and stood with me. The friends that mattered were also supportive and a huge weight was lifted from my shoulders.

During the few years that I lived behind the bar, I made sure my roommates were aware so that I wasn't living a lie in my own house. They all had zero problems with it. My mother was another story. Just when I thought she couldn't disappoint me any further, the way she chose to handle the news of my being gay was shocking. She bombarded me with terrible insults like, "Why can't you just spread your legs like the rest of us? No dyke is a daughter of mine!" The things she said were brutal and demoralizing. She drove to my apartment after being at the bar too long and pounded on my door in the middle of the night screaming, "Who's sleeping with who in there?" Obviously, I didn't answer the door and my straight roommate was astounded by the drama. Thankfully, my roommate understood my pain, anxiety, and embarrassment over my mother's behavior. The episodes converted to comic relief and we got a lot of laughs at Mom's expense. Of all people! I never thought she would have issues, being a hippie and all. I was under the impression that she experienced a woman back in the day, so why the dramatic outrage? She told Grandma Zofie which really pissed me off! If I lost favor with my beloved Grandma, I would kill her! Luckily for my mother, Grandma skirted the issue with a funny phone call saying, "Sylviaaa, I heard sumting. Is it chrew?" When I asked her what it was that she heard, she replied, "Oh . . . nutting. Naver mind." I was relieved! Now, I prayed my brother was not being subjected to the negative comments about me. What a nightmare.

Mom went into a phase of denial and blamed herself for the way I was, giving her an excuse to drink more. This charade went on for a couple of years, so I ignored her the best I could and decided to go back to college after the art degree didn't pay off. I studied Zoology and Animal Management, landing an awesome internship at the Zoo. It was the coolest thing I'd ever done! I worked with reptiles of every sort, birds of prey, rhinos, you name it, but my absolute favorites were the lions, tigers and leopards. The energy and satisfaction I encountered while working with them was breathtaking. Every day, I found myself in awe and respect of their beauty and ferociousness. Over time, Mom slowly came to terms with reality and we were able to have civil conversations about some of my neat experiences at the Zoo and it seemed we were slowly patching things up. I still didn't care to be around her while under the influence, so we chatted more when she was sober. As it finally dawned on her that being gay was not just a phase I was going through, her insults lessened.

When my mother witnessed a failed relationship that devastated me in my early twenties, she saw similarities between her and my dad and told me a story. "Your father was so smart! He was great looking, very kind, funny, and had friends that adored him. He was spiritual and seemed to have a certain wisdom about him. I loved him for ALL of it! And everything that I saw in your father was something that I wanted for myself. Sylvia, you are like your father. People are drawn to you and when they're around you long enough, they start comparing themselves to you. By no fault of his own, I felt totally insignificant inside when I was around him and I judged myself to be a failure. From what I've noticed, your girlfriend did the same and was so unhappy with herself that she bailed." Witness to her daughter's heartbreak, Mom realized that a relationship was a relationship. The love and the pain were all the same. I appreciated the fact that she was trying to give me comfort. I would keep this story in mind.

I loved my mother when she was sober. Conversations were deep and meaningful, clear and loving. I saw the rift between Mom and I slowly mending. This became very apparent to me one afternoon when I stopped by to visit. We sat and talked, while on the television was a lesbian fighting for custody of her child. Mom spoke up and said, "That's just terrible that they want to take her child away because she's in a gay relationship." Then she looked at me and said, "I've thought about it and you are my daughter no matter what! People shouldn't be condemned for who they are." I smiled and a wave of love washed over me. I hadn't felt that for her in years. I thought to myself, 'I'm finally getting my mother back!' She was beginning to cut down on the drinking and I was becoming less judgmental. Now I was rooting for her and hoped she could see better things for herself in a life of sobriety.

CHAPTER 6

AUTUMN MOLT

IT WAS IN EARLY September when Mom went to an oral surgeon to have all her teeth pulled due to periodontal disease. Her lifelong friend, Carly, was the designated driver and was taken aback by a statement my mother made on the way to surgery, "Deep down, I'm really scared, and I don't want to die." Carly asked her what she meant by that and Mom could only say that she was fearful right down to her core. The surgery needed to be done and as Carly reassured her, everything turned out fine.

Mom and I had a few laughs over her 'old lady' smile. It seemed so odd to see her without teeth at only forty-three years old. She was relieved that the surgery was over and hoped to heal fast and get fitted for dentures asap because every time she laughed, she put her hand to her mouth to cover herself. We definitely had fun joking about that, but for the first time, Mom wasn't telling me how she was feeling physically. This was unusual because she always had a complaint about something, to the point that I thought she was a hypochondriac. As the days passed, her health deteriorated.

Carly took Mom to her follow up dentist appointment and when everything seemed to check out well, Mom asked if they could stop at a store on the way home. She complained about some ailments as they pulled into the parking lot of a convenience store and when Carly saw my mother return to the car with beer, she noted, "Now that's not going to make you feel better!"

Mom shrunk with embarrassment, "I have to." It was then that Carly realized her best friend Sharon was an alcoholic. There were a few years lost between them when she was with Mario. Occasionally, they had phone conversations, but all of Mom's problems during the marriage were kept hidden and Carly had no idea.

The girls knew each other from way back and it was Carly that introduced my parents to one another. She dated my father. In later years she told me the story, with a gleam in her eye, describing how beautiful he was. She sat in a bar with a friend and noticed a man with gorgeous long hair walking into the bar across the street. She wanted to meet him, but she was too shy. Every time she went out to the bar, my father would appear across the street. Carly was completely taken by him and one day, gathered up the nerve to walk over to the other bar, finding him standing at the jukebox. She introduced herself, they talked, and started dating shortly thereafter. The relationship was short lived, but they remained friends. Leif introduced Carly to one of his best friends which turned out to be her life long husband. Carly, in turn, introduced her best friend, Sharon, to my father and the rest is history. Over the years Carly and her husband made the healthy decision to get away from the drug scene in order to survive; on an individual basis as well as for their relationship. Slowly they saw their friends dying or becoming addicts, unable to function in relationships. The only way out was to clean up and keep a safe distance. Sharon admired that about Carly and was proud and happy for both of them. She, on the other hand, was disconcerted by her dependency and hid it for years. At least now, she was being honest with her BFF.

The fear of death had not left my mother after the surgery and grew more intense. Sharon was getting sicker, complaining of stomach and abdominal problems. She told Carly she didn't know what was going on and thought that maybe she ate a bad piece of meat or something. She wasn't sure. Within a few days, I received a call from Grandma Zofie telling me that Mom was in the hospital. I automatically planned on going to her house to be there for my brother when he got out of school, but it was early, and I went directly to the intensive care unit to see her. When I arrived, they were running tests to figure out what was going on and I patiently waited. She looked at me with tears and desperation as she lay in the hospital bed and said, "The doctor doesn't know what's wrong and it's getting worse. He says it doesn't look good. I don't want to die!"

My first thoughts to this were, 'Are you crazy? You're just exaggerating!' Then I got mad and thought, 'What kind of shit is the doctor telling her when they don't even know what's wrong?' Seeing her in that bed made me a little scared. She mentioned my brother and I told her, "Already thought of that. I got it covered."

I needed the car keys to move her vehicle so that she wouldn't get a parking ticket and she pointed to her purse. I noticed a couple of bills in there and asked if she would like me to pay them for her. With a sharp snap she replied, "Don't touch anything or take my food stamps!"

I didn't understand why she lashed out at me like that and snapped back, "I'm just trying to do you a favor!" Her purse and clothes had to be put in a bag and sent to hospital check-in, and her bills would go unpaid. We ended with, "I'll see you later."

I met my brother at the house after school and told him about Mom in the hospital. I explained that we had to wait for test results to see what's going on. He seemed a little worried but said, "She will come home soon." I agreed. The following day, I went to the hospital alone and wasn't ready for what I saw. My mother transformed into something unrecognizable overnight. She doubled in size, was black and blue from head to toe, and was now wired up with tubes to a machine. Her eyes were open a quarter of the way and motionless. Motionless…in a coma. My chest grew tight as an overwhelming uneasiness consumed me. My hand covered my mouth as I cried, reaching out, "Mom? Mommy? What happened? What's going on?" Just then, the nurse came and shooed me out of the room telling me, "You shouldn't be in here. She's not ready yet." My heart sank, my mind was blown and I was completely pissed that I was asked to leave. "I'm not going anywhere. What happened?" She explained that these things sometimes happen with internal body fluid. She hadn't noticed me come in and wanted to take the time to prep me for what I was going to see. I had a lot of questions. What the hell was going on?

A few days passed and the doctors had no answer; only that she had a bladder infection. They were asking me questions about signing papers and told me that, being the eldest child, the decisions were mine. "What decisions?" They needed authorization in the event her heart stopped to resuscitate or not. All this happened so fast, my head was in a whirl wind and it seemed completely unreal. Confusion. Anger. Fear. Worry. How can this be? Again, what the hell is going on? I was being put on the spot to make these serious decisions and it seemed they were rushing for my answers. I needed to think and asked for a couple of days. They understood.

I went home that night feeling utterly alone and wanting to vomit. What is the right thing to do? What would Mom want? She had no will or healthcare proxy. She told me she didn't want to die but there was a twist here. She would not want to live her life as a vegetable, dependent on machines with absolutely no quality of life. This much I did know. Over the next two days, all her internal organs shut down with the exception of her heart and they STILL had no answers! The only thing they told me was the obvious. Her body went septic. They put her on a respirator and said the longer she stayed in a coma, the greater the chance she'd be brain damaged or even brain dead. What was I going to tell my little brother? I went into shock. Our mother is dying, and they don't know why. They can't fix her. Every day I asked what the chances of her waking up normal would be. At first it was 50/50. Then, 40/60, then 20/80 until finally they told me she would be brain dead. I signed the 'do not resuscitate' papers. All of this happened in just one week's time.

I had to put on a strong face. Everything was falling apart. Grandma Zofie was a mess, watching her child die. My uncle was in just as much a shock as I was. I thought long and hard about it and felt that my brother should be given the chance to see her. I wanted him to have the opportunity to tell her that he loved her and to say goodbye. I believe people in comas can hear us and I wanted my brother to understand this. I wondered if seeing her in this condition would scar him in some way. My intention was not to make it more painful for him, but if he was kept from his mother in her final days, what would he think for the rest of his life? Would he be angry and have hang-ups later on for not being able to say, "I Love You?" That wouldn't be right or fair. He would have hang-ups regardless. The next day I took him to the hospital. He was frightened and the reality was hitting him that maybe Mom wasn't coming home. I wrapped my arm tightly around him and walked slowly through the doorway. As we approached her, he shrank at the horrific sight, smell, and sounds of our mother's death bed. I told him she could hear us and had him say a few things to her. My eyes welled up with tears as I tried my damnedest to hold it together. I only made it through the day for him.

Finally, some test results were in and they came up with E. coli. For a moment, I had a glimmer of hope. Now they know what it is! Now they can cure it! But the damage was done. Nothing in her body worked anymore. Just her heart. If only they would have discovered the E. Coli earlier, they told me, there would have been a chance. My pulse stuttered, and the pressure in my head blew like a tea kettle, "What kind of medical staff is this?!" My knees weakened as I walked from the nurse's station into the room alone and talked to my mother. I held her. I cried. I stroked her face and lifted her eyelid, gazing into her still, hazel eye, hoping for a reaction. "I love you Mom." I told her what the doctors were telling me and about her being a vegetable. I said that I would take care of things, that she needn't worry and that it's okay for her to let go and not be afraid. God was there.

The next day I met Grandma and my uncle at the hospital. Mom's heart rate had become extremely erratic throughout the night and the nurse showed me the EKG printouts. It was very clear that this was it. I went to her side and placed one hand on her head and my other held her hand. Grandma stood behind me while my uncle tried holding it together on the other side of the bed. We listened to her heart monitor with tears in our eyes. The sound …bleeps …sporadic and climbing faster and faster. We held her. Her brother hopelessly called her name, "Sharon!" Grandma was crying as she whimpered, "No! Don't go." I cried, "Mom", as the bleeps turned to a steady, almost endless monotone and she died in our arms. I sensed that Grandma should stand where I was to be close to Mom's face. I put my arm around her and then moved out of the way. She grabbed her daughter, "Sharon? No! No! Sharon!" Holding my mother, she wept. I lost it. I didn't know what was worse. Losing your mother or losing your child. I not only grieved for myself but for Grandma too. My mind was in a whirl. How was I going to . . . what was I . . . I can't believe this happened!

It was hard for any of us to leave. We would have to. Just a couple more minutes. Even though she was gone, there was an eerie feeling that she was still with us as her chest rose and fell. Mom was still attached to the respirator and I hoped by some miracle it would breathe life back into her. The nurse in the room was teary-eyed as she walked over to the machine and unplugged it. Silence.

I walked out to the nurse's station and asked what I needed to do now. It was explained that I get her bag of personal belongings from the basement storage area. The nurse was shaken up and touched by my loss. She told me, it was like Mom fought and waited until we got there before letting go. She had several attacks throughout the night and should've passed, but it wasn't until we stood and held her. I thanked the nurse for sharing that with me.

Grandma and I shuffled our feet, embraced in each other's arms as we headed for the elevator. My name was called from behind us and I turned to see the doctor. He asked if I wanted an autopsy done. Grandma sobbed and in a broken voice said, "Doan cut her up. She's been chrew enough." What was left of my heart sank into my stomach. Seeing Grandma Zofie cry was devastating to me. The decision was mine and I wanted the autopsy, but I didn't want to go against my grandmother's wishes. Up until now, she had absolutely no say in anything. I declined out of respect for her and signed the last paper. When we got down to the first floor, Grandma and I parted ways and I went to the storage area. It hurt to say her name at the desk for retrieval. Mom's voice echoed in my head as I saw the two unpaid bills in her purse. My despair dulled me into a zombie-like state as my legs somehow carried me outside the hospital. The air was strange. Everything looked thick and yellow. This weird atmosphere put me into a twilight zone of sorts and I found myself walking aimlessly down the street. I bumped into somebody I knew and said that I just lost my mother a half hour ago. I don't remember the rest of the conversation or the drive home. I don't know how I got to the funeral parlor to pick out a casket, dress, hairstyle, and news write-up. I don't remember how I told my brother or his father that he was now staying with. I only remember a hollow nothingness.

The following day, while I was busy making funeral arrangements, my little brother called and asked if he could come live with me. I carefully explained that his dad had the say in the matter. I wasn't home much, being a twenty-four year old young adult working at a bar and going to school fulltime. I barely made enough money to take care of myself and when I tried to tell him this, he melted my heart by saying, "I could get a paper route so I could help buy food." He sounded so desperate and I wanted nothing more than to say yes, but I knew his father would never let it happen. Mario hated me and when he caught wind of my sexuality, it made things worse. I felt helpless and didn't want to let him down after all we'd been through, but he was asking the impossible. When we hung up the phone, sorrow possessed me like a demon and I was inconsolable.

The next few days were difficult. I tried as hard as I could to keep my chin up to comfort my brother and Grandma. The thought of having to deal with everything after the funeral was exhausting and I gladly accepted the hugs from all who came and paid their respects. Seeing Mom's old friends from years past was both soothing and agonizing at the same time. All those years, good and bad, long gone. I realized that day how much my mother was loved, even with all her faults, by everyone. I knew that after today, I would not see some of these people ever again. They were time travelers, linked to me through my mother. From the land of ago, they appeared, cried with me, said goodbye, disappeared, and returned to the back of my memory where they are preserved for all time.

This was a time of change; a time of major hurt and turmoil which later became motivation for me to strive for inner peace and true joy. But until then, I dealt with more hell on earth. I contacted Mom's landlord and said I would pay another month's rent to buy some time to pack up her apartment. He was understanding and agreed. My little brother was brought over for the first time to get his things and when he walked in, he was a changed boy, full of dejection and anger. I could see that something had disconnected. We packed his clothes and his father had enough room to take a mirror and dresser. I looked at my brother and said I would pack up all his toys with the rest of his bedroom and bring it over another day. He loved his GI Joe stuff and had every action figure, car, and command center available. He gazed around the room for a moment and then looked at the floor. "I don't want any of it." There was a coldness in him that sent chills through my spine. I understood his pain and thought he would change his mind eventually, so I left it alone.

Mom didn't have much, just the basic necessities and a car that was in dire need of repair. There was no money in the bank. In fact, she was two dollars overdrawn. The plan was to keep anything sentimental or useful to me and my brother and then have a small estate sale. One day, as I was packing up, her phone rang and it was her divorce lawyer. I can't recall exactly what he wanted. I imagine it was about trying to go after Mario for child support payments which were tens of thousands in arrears. When I broke the news to the lawyer about Mom, he asked a lot of questions. As I was right in the middle of packing up, he instructed me to put a halt on everything, "These matters need to be dealt with properly and legally." When I explained to him that Mom had absolutely nothing of value and further expressed confusion and hesitance as to why he needed to be involved, he insisted. The lawyer made it sound like I would be breaking the law if I took care of things on my own. So, against my will, I complied with what he said. When I contacted Mom's landlord and gave him the update, he said I could have the place as long as necessary. I made sure he was paid.

I resumed my college classes and focused on getting my life back in order while I waited for further instructions from the lawyer. Two weeks went by before I returned to her apartment. I didn't want things to drag out, but in a way, it was nice to have a break. I took care of some personal odds and ends: grocery shopping, doctor appointments and the like. It was then that a seed was planted in my head that made me question everything.

I had a great relationship with my dentist and he was always curious to hear updates about my colorful life. I shared what happened with my mother and he listened intensely. The matter was sketchy to me as everything happened so fast and I described the horrible and confusing days of not having answers until it was too late. He was truly sorry for my loss, expressed disbelief and a hint of anger as he wished to share his opinion with me. What I heard from him made me wish I had gone with my gut and had the autopsy done.

It was only a theory, but by the way things happened, he seemed to think she was introduced to E. Coli via her oral surgery. It wasn't long after that when she got sick and the situation spun out of control. He said, very candidly and with strong concern, "It sounds to me like somebody took a shit and didn't wash their hands before working on your Mom." So much bacteria can be introduced to the body through dentistry and this idea wasn't far-fetched. My chest caved and my mind endlessly wondered. As soon as I got home, I forwarded this possibility to the lawyer and, naturally, he showed great interest, "We'll tidy up the estate and begin an investigation into her death." I said I had no money to pay him but he told me not to worry; we would work something out. For a moment, I was excited about the lawyer! He knew Grandpa Loosha, which is how Mom found him. He most certainly helped HER, so maybe he will do the same for me. With that, I set my concerns aside and headed over to my mother's place.

Mom lived above a pizza parlor, owned by her landlord, and he was usually there. I was glad to know where to look for him because, upon arrival to the apartment, my key didn't work. At first, I thought, 'Did I bring the wrong key? How. . . no . . .this is it. This is the right one. What's going on? I guess I'll go downstairs and get him.' To my dismay, he wasn't there so I left a message for him to contact me. For days, I tried to reach him by phone with no response. I drove by the pizza shop numerous times and, one day, noticed a sign in the window that said, 'Apartment for Rent'. I grew suspicious and called Grandma Zofie, explaining my dilemma. She put in a call to her sister Gina and they devised a plan to check it out. Grandma and I couldn't do anything because the landlord knew who we were, but he didn't know Gina!

Grandma's sister called the number on the 'for rent' sign and set up an appointment to check out the apartment. He took the bait and the three of us hopped into Grandma's car one night to complete our mission. We parked across the street at the convenience store and Gina went out to meet the landlord at the pizza shack. I was excited to play 'undercover spy' with Grandma as we tried to remain unseen, peering intensely through the car window. She was brilliant! Absolutely brilliant and I loved her for it! Now, we would find out what the hell was going on! Gina and the landlord were now standing in front of the building, having a conversation. Suddenly, they got into his truck and started the engine. WTF! As they drove past us, Gina shot us a wide-eyed glance. She was sending a signal that something went awry.

Grandma and I got out of the car and watched the truck disappear down the street, completely stupefied. Now what? We were worried for Gina but could do nothing but sit and wait. After a time, they returned, had a couple words and parted ways. When Gina got back to the car, she explained that the sign was for a different apartment. To not look suspicious, she had to play along and go for the ride, making small talk. He asked her a bunch of questions like, why are you moving, do you have children, etc. etc. She almost panicked when he asked where she parked so that she could follow him to the apartment, but being quick on your toes runs in the family! "My son dropped me off and will be back shortly." He then asked if she was interested in the rental. Gina explained that because of where the sign was posted, it was assumed that the apartment was in that building and she liked the location. He mentioned that, eventually, he would have a vacancy so she expressed great interest and asked why. "The woman there died," he said. Gina expressed her condolences, asked what happened, and he replied, "Oh, it was some drunk." After listening to my aunt's story, all my Grandma could say was, "Watt an asshoe!" We drove home, thanking Gina for what she had done for us.

That bastard! It wasn't until he received a threatening message from the lawyer that he stopped avoiding me. The next time I drove over to the pizza place, I found him. He was surprised to see me and seemed very annoyed with my presence. When I asked what was up with Mom's house being locked, he told me the place had been rented. My blood came to a boil and I responded, "Number one . . . there were still days left in the month that were paid for and, number two . . . we had an understanding that I would continue to pay until all was settled!" Then, I questioned where my mother's belongings were as daggers shot from my eyes. His response was, "I put all of her shit in the attic." I glared at him and insisted that he best give me access!

Straight away, we headed upstairs and as he unlocked the door, he informed me that the new tenants turned out to be trash. "They moved in, and then moved out overnight," as he opened the door. As I walked in, I noticed Mom's curtains still dressed the windows but nothing else remained. He escorted me to a door with a padlock and told me he did this to keep my mother's things safe. I eagerly went upstairs and he pointed me to the front of the attic. I scanned the area and there weren't many items that looked even faintly familiar. "What about her bed? Dressers? Kitchen table? Washer and dryer? Her clothes? Where are all my brother's toys? Where is EVERYTHING?" I found two boxes in the entire attic that were hers and they were ransacked. My mind was murderous as I belted out a verbal lashing. He made matters worse when he acted as if he didn't know what happened. "Maybe that's why the new tenants took off. They saw all this stuff, well taken care of, and exchanged their garbage for her things."

The story about the padlock on the attic door to protect her things was an obvious lie. The whole thing was a scandal. I'm sure there were no "mystery tenants". Out of my wits, I called and notified the lawyer of my findings. The stress came to a climax and I burned out, spiraling into a deep depression. To top it off, the lawyer called and said he needed some money to continue the legal proceedings before the court date when the landlord would appear and answer to the charges. I reminded the lawyer of our prior conversations, telling him I had no money and that he was aware of that fact. Then, on the other end of the phone, I heard, "You could pay me in bed."

Not believing my ears, I snapped, "WHAT?" He didn't repeat himself. My patience was long gone and it could be heard in my voice, "I don't know what sorts of arrangements you make with people but let me make it clear that I have NOTHING to offer! You are the one who caused this entire mess! It was your idea to hold everything up, and for what?" He quickly responded, saying that things were in motion, needed to be followed through, and asked if there was anyone who could give me money for him, like my grandmother. In full blown assault, I let him have it, "You made this mess, not me! I didn't want to deal with you at all! My mother didn't have much and yet you insisted on getting involved and now there's NOTHING AT ALL! I'm done with you! You figure it out!" I slammed the phone down and never spoke to him again.

A few weeks later, I received a letter from the lawyer's office containing the results of action taken against Mom's landlord. They quickly finished up in small claims court and mailed me a check for three hundred bucks.

I regretted answering the phone that day at Mom's apartment while I was packing her things. All would have been fine without that stupid, greedy, perverted, opportunist of a lawyer. It wasn't about the money. I knew her things didn't have much monetary value. It was about what was lost. . . taken from my brother and me. It was so devastating! I don't know how I got through it. Somehow, thankfully, the universe carried me.

School kept my mind occupied, though I admit it was hard to concentrate at times. I would be graduating in a few months which gave me something to look forward to …something to be proud of. I wanted to feel good …feel like something mattered. I needed a break from all the bad shit and Ma Bitar came through with an opportunity. I was asked to give drug speeches to seventh and eighth graders preparing for high-school and, desperate for distraction and purpose, I eagerly agreed. I shared stories of my "party days", experimenting with just about everything, having a close call with death, and described the horror of being on a bad acid trip. I explained the circumstances surrounding my father's lethal overdose and, with tears in my eyes, discussed the recent death of my alcoholic mother. I knew the message wouldn't reach everyone and I was a little unnerved with all those eyes staring at me in judgement. Yet, I hoped it would help at least a couple of young people. Years later, I was happy to hear that it did. I was approached by a man that remembered me from that day. He shared, "I just wanted to let you know that what you said made a difference." I am so thankful for that!

CHAPTER 7

ENDURING THE WINTER

MA AND DAD BITAR attended my graduation, along with my new girlfriend. I felt empty that day and it meant so much to have support. Tears ran down my cheek as I sat thinking about my mother, waiting for my name to be called to walk across the stage and receive my diploma. I knew I was surrounded by good people; classmates, friends, and an extended family that cared for me deeply. They turned my melancholy into a day of celebration. Through it all, I persevered and gave myself a pat on the back for completing the program, to earn another degree.

Soon after graduation, I went to my mother's grave and talked to her. I gave her an update on everything as I hovered with slumped shoulders on one knee in the dirt, smoking a cigarette. A breeze blew softly as I looked to the sky and asked for a sign of acknowledgement. I looked back at the headstone and an annoying fly kept buzzing around my hand. I waved it away several times as I continued having a discussion with the ground. The bug was persistent and landed on my hand, so I gave up and let it sit there as I cried. It flew up in front of my face and back to my hand several times, as if to get my attention. Curious, I paused, silenced myself, and looked more closely at this fly on my hand. There was something comforting about it and I took my index finger and moved slowly to gently pet its wings. I was astonished that it let me and didn't fly away! Lifting my hand close to my face, it turned to look me in the eye. "Mom? Is that you?" I laughed and said, "Geez! I guess you really fucked up if you came back as a house fly!" My heart felt like a feather and that fly stayed on my hand for most of the drive home. I was never so tickled! I would look at house flies completely differently from then on.

Back at home, my roommate and I both had a job lined up at the local Zoo. We performed well while completing our internship during the past two years and were taken on as seasonal workers. That summer, we worked the camel rides and a children's petting zoo. On rainy days, if I was lucky, I had the opportunity to revisit the lions and tigers. THAT was what I really wanted to do! The chance to be close to these exotic creatures was awe-inspiring and took my mind off how backbreaking some of the work really was. Essentially, I was a glorified shit shoveler but couldn't be happier when I was in the company of the great cats. The pay was terrible with no benefits, but I stuck it out in the hopes of being taken on permanently. This meant health insurance and more pay. By the end of the season, they only offered seasonal status again. According to the full-time keepers, the Zoo did this all the time to avoid paying out more. I was disappointed because I had passed up an opportunity for a huge sum of money that would have proven very useful. Early in the season, I was head-butted by a camel during an after-hours company picnic. The impact shattered my front teeth and I received a serious concussion, all because the illiterate jackass in charge did not heed my many warnings to take the agitated animals back to their enclosures. The temptation to sue The Zoo was huge, but I was told that if I did that, I would never get a job in any zoo anywhere. I settled for having my teeth fixed.

It was my own fault, assuming I would be offered a permanent position after the summer season. I somehow thought The Zoo would take care of me after my accident, but I was sadly mistaken. If I had been willing to relocate to somewhere like San Diego or Columbus, perhaps I would still be a zoo keeper. I sent out some inquiries but didn't pursue anything. My motivation to relocate was almost nonexistent. Perhaps I was afraid to venture out into the world alone. I had a deep emptiness in my heart and couldn't bear the thought of leaving Grandma, my brother, the Bitar's, and my friends. I needed familiarity and that kept me bound. I became a pet groomer that year and moved back to the suburbs. My friends joked with me when they found out my new address was 666. I'd been through so much, as if cursed, and now I was living in the "devil's" house. This was all nonsense, of course, but we had a good laugh. Moving back placed me closer to my brother and the Bitar's. The apartment was small, but I loved it! My drum set wouldn't fit, so the Bitar's let me keep it in their basement. This was the first time I had lived completely alone in years and I honored it as my own personal sanctuary. It was here that I started burning a lot of incense while listening to guided meditation CD's. I discovered tons of New Age and World music which inspired me to sit, relax, reflect, write more often, and pick up my musical instruments every once in a while.

I played the guitar for years but always had a strong desire for percussion. I have a memory of being introduced to the drums when I was about two-years-old. My mom took me to some party and there was a band playing in the basement. She carried me down the steps, placed me on my feet, and my attention was immediately drawn to the drum kit. Without any thought, I wobbled over slowly, noticing the guitar players in my peripheral vision, never taking my eye off the target. I approached the drummer and he put me on is lap, placing the sticks in my hands and assisted me in hitting the tom-toms. The experience moved me and the desire to play remained. I got a used kit while living behind the bar and taught myself how to play. The joy that filled me from drumming was incredible! I was thankful for being able to visit my kit and play them at the Bitar's.

It was great to be back here, though I thought I'd never say that. Many times, I had been consumed with the big city and had longings to return because my earliest roots were there. I dwelled on the past frequently and longed for those good years with Mom and her friends. The years spent with her bad marriage and alcohol abuse were scars on my mind that I wanted to forget, and I tried only thinking of the happy, early memories. The hopes that she would find herself were decimated. Sorrow crept in sometimes and I used to cry for me, but now, I cried for her in what seemed to be an incredibly tragic life-story right to the end. Being back in town brought on some of these negative images. This was where many terrible things happened, and I started meditating more frequently to find peace. Everything happened for a reason and it was here in this town, amongst the pain, that I met some of the most important people in my life. When I focused on the 'good', it started to feel like home again. I continued to be involved with the softball league and steered clear of drugs. I focused on my meditations which drew out an understanding and thankfulness inside of me for all the trauma I had experienced. I was learning to see things differently.

I had an eagerness to declutter, ridding my life of negativity as much as possible, and would be given this opportunity through the actions of the woman I was dating at the time. She was beautiful, seemed kind and thoughtful; coming from a caring family; and I thought she was a good catch until I discovered her true colors. One particular evening, she wanted to go out drinking and I was fine with that, as long as she didn't come to my house afterwards. I had to work in the morning and knew she would get totally plowed and want to show up in the middle of the night, disrupting my sleep. She agreed with my request and went on her way. As I lay in a deep slumber under my blanket at three in the morning, I was abruptly awoken by slaps and punches to the body and head. At first, I thought there was a break-in and I was about to be raped and killed. I struggled, getting tangled up in the blanket, and as I heard the cursing, I then realized it was my drunk girlfriend trying to catch me in bed with someone else. When she didn't find what she conjured up in her mind, she became enraged for not having a reason to leave me. As I flip-flopped, attempting to free myself, I said in a low and gravelly voice, "If I get out of this bed, I'm gonna kill you!" (Not meaning this literally, of course). She kept coming at me and I maneuvered my way to the opposite end of the bed and freed myself. I leaped up and charged her, blocking her flailing arms and locked her in a bear hug. "Calm down! It's ok. If you want to hit me, hit me now and get it out of your system." Her arms clumsily hit the sides of my body until she tired and could fuss no more. She started crying and said she wanted to have a reason to walk away from the relationship, but could find none. I was confused with her irrationality.

No, she didn't have a reason, but I DID and would do her a favor! I was tired of her weekend drinking binges and flirtation with anybody but me. I released the bear-hug, thinking it was safe, and told her to go home. She stumbled through the kitchen towards the door and, without warning, proceeded to shatter my dishes, waking my neighbors. The only thing on my mind was my cats cutting their paws on the broken glass. This bitch was out of control and I had to put an end to it, so I sprinted to the kitchen and wrestled her to the floor, all the while telling her to knock it off and get out! When she started yelling and throwing punches, I sat on her stomach, put my hands around her throat and squeezed as hard as I could, "Just stop it and get the fuck out of here!" The fury consumed me as I looked at her face, now purple. A flash from the past hit me like a truck and all I saw was Mario strangling my mother. I instantly let go and got up, telling myself she wasn't worth it. I called the cops to have her removed. I knew right then; the past trauma had saved me from making a terrible mistake. She was an unhealthy person and I had to gather enough love for myself to not allow anyone to do to me what my mother had permitted. I was mad at myself for believing her apology and hanging around for another couple of weeks, only to receive a literal slap in the face in my own home again. I was done! I cared for her, but the help she needed was beyond my power.

It was right around this time when I was asked to play in a band. I met some nice people and was enjoying my new-found freedom at a local gay bar. One of the girls wanted to start an all-female band and approached me to ask if I played any musical instruments. I told her I'd been playing guitar for years but also was teaching myself how to play drums, though I didn't think I was good at it yet. She said to me, "Which one do you really love?"

My choice was easy, "The drums!" Confidence in my abilities was low, but I had to take a chance! By the time we got everything together, there were eight of us vigorously practicing. We had two guitars, bass, keyboards, drums, saxophone, harmonica and vocals. Surprisingly, we were quite popular and packed every place we played. The band got a lot of press; getting our names and pictures in the paper with rave reviews. I developed strong ties with these girls and though our personalities would clash on occasion, it was invigorating! The project lasted about two years before we couldn't stand to be in the same room with each other anymore. But that was OK. It was time to move on anyways and this playing experience opened the door to future bands for me.

As full as my schedule was, I still made time to talk to Grandma Zofie every day on the phone, drive over to see her when I could, and take her to Bingo. After a while, I couldn't help but notice her forgetfulness. When she called my residence and got the answering machine, she'd leave a message to return her call when I got in. Then, as if she didn't remember, she dialed me every ten minutes for the next few hours, completely filling up the tape on my answering machine with her cute voice.

Grandma had owned a beauty salon for decades. She was now in her early eighties, but refused to retire. The salon was near her home and she drove herself there every day at about six in the morning and stayed until three or four in the afternoon. Over time, as the business slowed down, I think she called me from work just for something to do. On her days off, she REALLY blew up my phone and most of her voice mails were repetitive. No one else could leave a message for me because my damn machine was constantly full! But it was nice to know that Grandma thought about me all the time. We enjoyed each other's company and I couldn't get mad at her for wanting to go to dinner or Bingo.

On Saturdays, Grandma's sister Auntie Hattie would keep her busy. Since I was a little girl, Grandma picked her sister up early in the morning once a week before work and dropped her off at the house to clean all day. When Grandma Zofie got home, they would eat whatever homemade dinner Hattie prepared and then they were off to Bingo before Grandma took her home. Auntie Hattie never learned how to drive and cleaning house for Grandma may have been one of her only jobs. As she cleaned, she always hummed a cheerful tune and laughed at Grandpa Loosha's light-heartedness as he relentlessly joked, poked, and teased her. I loved when he picked on her to get a reaction and I looked forward to her visits.

Though we visited all of Grandma's sisters, I was closest to Hattie. It was she, that informed me at a family funeral that Grandma's driving was getting bad. Hattie was now afraid to drive anywhere with her because she was cutting corners a little to close and lightly sideswiping guard rails or telephone poles. As I recalled Grandma complaining about her vehicle, "Dose damn kids scratchin up my car! You can't have any ting nice," things were now making sense. Dementia! The rest of her sisters chimed in and said her mind was going. I voiced the idea that perhaps I should move in and help her out, but had to put some serious thought into it. I loved my apartment and my freedom. I was in the prime of my life at around twenty-six-years-old and I don't know many people who would've given up their youthful years to care for an elderly person. This would be a big job! On the other hand, I loved my Grandma and it seemed the right thing to do; something I would not regret. After all, she took care of me and now I could return the favor. I made up my mind and all her sisters rejoiced and applauded my decision.

When I ran the idea by Grandma about moving in, she was ecstatic! I would set up my 'apartment' in her basement to be surrounded by some of my things and have a little privacy. It was larger than my current apartment, so I could fit my drums down there too! As I set up shop, Grandma noticed my three cats and was not very happy with that. She never cared for house pets, but I reassured her that they would live down there with me and she didn't have to worry, or be afraid of them. Eventually, she warmed up and talked to them. To my surprise, she even played with them once or twice.

It didn't take long to settle in. This was the house where I grew up and it truly felt like home. Here we go again, back to the city, but I knew I belonged here with Grandma. She and I always had a special bond and now we were growing even closer, almost inseparable. When we got home from work, we talked, ate dinner, and watched TV together. Every day it was the six-o-clock news followed by Wheel of Fortune and Jeopardy. We frequented Bingo, of course, and I took her out to dinner, visiting family, church functions, and summer field days, just to name a few. I chauffeured her around, for our own safety, and she repeatedly told me she liked my driving, "Yewd be a goot race car driver!" I smiled every time she said it! I took over some of the chores like cutting the grass, shoveling snow, food shopping, cooking more often, and cleaning the house. Auntie Hattie decided it would be a good time to retire now that I was living there again. I'd miss seeing her ever Saturday …miss playing old songs on the organ for her as she sang in Polish, but I couldn't blame her for dreading a car ride with Grandma. If only Grandpa Loosha were still alive to pick her up!

The next year was sad and frustrating, watching Grandma slowly decline right in front of my eyes. She repeated herself, asking the same questions over and over again. I was pretty good at handling it at first, but now she was starting to get under my skin and my patience was wearing down. My day at work as a pet grooming manager was long and sometimes backbreaking. When I came home, my second shift started and most days I truly looked forward to bed-time. This was my Mecca, my comfort and escape, my favorite time of day. I had a waveless waterbed that was SO comfy, I would fall asleep almost immediately. Grandma wanted me to sleep upstairs and would ask, "Why do you sleep in da basement?" This was one of those reoccurring questions that I kindly answered the same way every day, "I love sleeping on my waterbed!"

Her response was also the same, "Waterbed? Ha do you sleep on dat? Who ever heard of such a ting?" Every time, I laughed and said, "Come on …I'll tuck you in," and would walk up to her room, help get her pajamas on and swing her legs up onto the mattress, which would make her giggle. I'd tell her I loved her and give her a kiss goodnight. "I luff you too," she replied as I turned out the light and retreated to my sanctuary.

Exhausted, I fed my soul by taking a few minutes to hang with my cats before passing out. In the middle of the night, I began to stir in my sleep, hearing shuffling noises in the dark. Suddenly, a bright beam of light covered my face, temporarily blinding me. Startled, I jumped up yelling, "What the hell!" preparing myself to beat the shit out the burglar. Then, a small, sweet Polish voice sounded from behind the light, "Watt are you doin' down here? Why doan you com upstairs?" I was infuriated! "What are you doing? Why did you wake me up? I have to get up early for work! Go back up to bed!" I felt bad for getting angry with her, but this went on for weeks! One night, I thought I was dreaming of the warm tropical sun and it turned out to be the flashlight in my face. Another time, I was awoken by hearing my name being called from the side of the bed and then, "Why do you let da cats sleep in da bed?"

I learned to expect her nightly visits and slept lightly, now able to catch her sneaking down the stairs way before she reached me across the room. Sometimes she tried to outwit me and left the flashlight behind. All I heard were slippers shuffling across the floor …closer …and CLOSER to the bed …her nose breathing heavily …exhale …inhale …exhale …trying to find me in the dark. "I hear you, Grandma!" Part of me thought about giving in and sleeping upstairs, but I knew that having my own space to regroup was paramount. Most of my day was consumed with Grandma and it was heartbreaking to witness her deterioration. She graduated to potty accidents; either soiling her pants or misfiring on the toilet and I now wiped and bathed her frequently. I knew I was slowly losing her and definitely needed my time-out space to cry.

Grandma Zofie could be a stubborn woman but that was getting worse as well. She didn't want to retire from her beauty salon and refused to stop driving. Her doctor insisted we get rid of her car and she was irate! I understood why. All her life, she had been a strong and independent spirit who looked out for herself. To take away her car and her work was like someone pulling the plug from her life. She was forgetful, yes, but had not completely lost her mind. So how could I blame her? I would fight too!

There was no question that Grandma's driving was dangerous, and my uncle sold her vehicle to the next-door neighbor. I wished that he would've taken more time to find a different buyer so that she wouldn't be reminded of her car every day. This was a thorn in her side and every time I took her to and from work, her frustration and anger was taken out on me. I was on her side, but she forgot to see that I was trying to help her. Grandma started calling family members, telling them that I didn't do anything around the house, the refrigerator was always empty, and that she was left alone all the time. I finally saw the nasty side of Grandma; the side I only heard rumors about, causing her and Grandpa to fight all the time. This eye-opener slapped me in the face, yet I stood my ground, knowing that dementia sends people into regression.

What appalled me was the nasty phone calls I received from the family. They had NO idea what was going on and didn't offer to help either! I had a heated conversation with my uncle about cutting the grass. I tried explaining that it was cut once a week, and Grandma would forget and want it cut two days later. She was obsessed with it! My uncle took grandma's side at first, not believing one word I had to say. I was furious for having to explain myself, "I've been here for over a year taking care of YOUR mother. No one has any idea what I'm dealing with. If you came around more, perhaps you would understand!" I hung up on him and felt good about what I said and hoped it would open his eyes a little bit.

Sometimes, raising one's voice seemed the only way to get heard around here! I assumed he was bothered by the constant and nagging phone calls from Grandma. She used to blow up my phone all the time. And perhaps he wasn't around much because he had good reason to separate himself. Growing up with my young grandparents was no treat for him and there were more bad memories than good. A close, warm and loving childhood did not exist for him. I don't think he wanted to deal with any of this, or at the very least, didn't know how to.

The next family phone call was from Grandma's oldest sister Carol. All geared up to give me a piece of her mind, she lashed, "Da last time I spoke wit Zofie, dare were only saltine crackers for dinner! Watt da hell is goin on over dare!" I calmly acknowledged her concern and reassured her that I was not starving the most beloved person in my life. There was always food in the house, but because of more recent developments, I was shopping more frequently rather than completely packing the freezer with months-worth of food, as it had always been.

My grandparents kept a room filled with food in canning jars, grown on the farm years ago. There were two full size freezers in the basement stuffed with deer meat from hunting and more farm veggies from fifteen years ago! Nothing was airtight, all was freezer burnt and not edible. I had to throw it all out. Knowing that Grandma's sister was old-school, she would not understand this and curse me for throwing out perfectly good food. I chose not to share that part of the story. What I did tell her provided a clear picture of what was happening. I had gone shopping after work and spent hundreds of dollars on meat for the freezer. I packed it tight with family sized packages of all Grandma's favorites; pork chops, polish sausage, chicken, hamburger, roasts, and ham. Just like Grandpa, it was easier for me to stock up for a month and buy in bulk so that shopping wouldn't become a hassle amidst juggling all my responsibilities.

One Sunday morning, I slept in until around 9am and as I headed for the bathroom, I smelled something delicious coming from upstairs. 'Grandma must be making breakfast or something,' I thought as I began to salivate. Then another thought occurred to me. The last time she cooked, she walked out of the room, forgot about the stove, and started a fire. Luckily, I was home from work and discovered the flames before any real damage was done. "Oh shit," as I climbed the stairs, curious and worried.

The aroma grew stronger with each ascending step and when I opened the door to peer in the kitchen, I was relieved to see Grandma standing at the cook top, tending to her frying pans.

"Good morning," I said as I looked around and noticed that every single burner had a pot or pan going with something different in each one. I peered into the wall mounted oven and discovered huge roasting pans baking. This scene looked familiar and I asked her what she was doing.

"Da family is comin' today!"

I sighed, "Grandma. What day do you think it is?"

When she told me it was Christmas, I looked around the kitchen and realized that every last bit of meat I bought, for the entire month, was now cooking. When I informed her that the family wasn't coming today she scowled and snapped, "Watt are you talkin about?" I told her to look outside and check for snow. The sun shone brightly down through the trees in the yard and bathed the blooming rose bushes. "Grandma …it's July."

Aunt Carol couldn't believe her ears when I finished telling her this. I reminded her that all the sisters, including her, practically begged me to come and take care of Grandma because they knew her mind was slipping. I had done that and these phone calls from the family were totally out of line. "Please take this information and let your sisters know the truth!"

Grandma's dementia got even worse, which was taking a toll on me physically and emotionally. At work, I stepped down from my managerial position to have more time with Grandma. I found myself trying to leave early all the time, constantly worried about leaving her alone. The neighborhood was changing drastically and she was robbed in her beauty salon after being knocked to the floor, breaking the glasses on her face. When she was home, she couldn't sit still and got into all kinds of trouble around the house. One time she wandered off, trying to walk to the salon on her day off and she was mugged. Her purse was stolen and a neighbor told me she was dropped off in front of the house by some stranger. She had a fat lip and scratches all over her arms from the bushes she was thrown into after being punched.

These things enraged me. I never understood why the older folks in my family were so negative towards the changing neighborhood and I fought tooth and nail not to be judgmental. But eventually, after witnessing my grandmother deal with being beaten and robbed several times throughout the years, I became angry in a way that I had previously thought only belonged to older and less educated generations. Every day, something terrible happened in our area and the news was full of sad happenings. I thought to myself, "Why are the people around here so bad?" I began to understand how anger and shortsightedness could spark wars. Seeing my grandma's victimization put a bad taste in my mouth. I saw how often the elderly were targets. They worked hard for what they had and others just took from them because it was easy. Some people are just plain shitty and I wondered if this would ever change.

I noticed an unfamiliar frailty developing in Grandma. For a moment, I wished that her dementia would serve to be useful …that she would forget about being angry and afraid of being alone. I hated seeing her like that! She was always tough as nails and had the ability to bounce back almost immediately. I worried for her and when I urged her to close up shop and retire after the last robbery and assault, she suddenly remembered her stubbornness and said, "Deez tings juss happen. For all da years I was in business, I was akchewly lucky to be robbed only a small handful a times. I have an obligation to my employees and customers. Besides, watt would I do all day long?" I would find this out.

Grandma's most loyal employee had been with her for decades. One day, she informed me that Grandma was losing her ability to use the scissors. This was not good news. Business had slowed down tremendously and more money was paid out for supplies, rent and bills than what was coming in. The fact that she refused to raise her prices higher than six dollars a cut didn't help. The going rate was double that in most other places, but Grandma was afraid her customers would go somewhere else if they had to pay more. The business had been losing money for the past few years. Many of her clients were either were dying off or not healthy enough to venture out anymore. A couple of Grandma's employee's left and took people with them. But paying to keep the shop open wasn't about the money anymore. It was about independence, pride, and socialization. This place was her lifeline. I knew that without it she would wither away, so for a while, I continued taking her there every morning at 6am and picking her up after I got out of work. When she was there, she usually stayed put as I called her throughout the day to check in on her. To try and avoid another robbery, I told her to keep the salon door locked and have the customers knock on the days her employee was not there with her.

Most days now, she had only one appointment but insisted she be there to answer the phone. I think she did a lot of snoozing in her chair when she wasn't spending time dialing wrong numbers to get a hold of her sisters to chat. One day I had a conversation on the phone with a stranger saying, "The same woman keeps calling and asking for Carol." I apologized and briefly explained the situation. The nice stranger understood. This provided me with the knowledge that Grandma was playing with the phone ALL day long.

Things escalated and Grandma Zofie became unpredictable and could not be left alone at all. She started walking home from the beauty shop before I got out of work and was forgetting to lock the door behind her. When she was home, she constantly set off the house alarm. On one of Grandma's days off, my girlfriend wanted me to go with her to her mom's house after work. I said it wasn't a good idea and I needed to go right home. She was aware of Grandma's condition but gave me a hard time anyways. It seemed to me that she was feeling annoyed and rejected by the amount of attention, love, care, and concern I was paying my grandmother. Our relationship was getting rocky and she craved all of my spare time, but I could not give what I didn't have. If I was lucky enough to get a moment, I just wanted to be left alone and not have to listen to constant talking. It was maddening! This particular day, as she continued to pester and nag me all day to go with her to her mother's, I just wanted her to shut up, so I agreed to go for an hour. Of course, she planned much more time than that and didn't get me home until after dark. I was so pissed! The whole time I was stressed out and my girlfriend claimed to understand, but she had NO idea!

As we pulled into the driveway and exited the car, I heard a small faint voice. At first, I thought it was coming from the front bushes. I paused and had to tell the girlfriend to be quiet and listen. "Help me," it said, and my first instinct was that someone was trying to lure me into the bushes. I slowly walked towards the house, "Halp me. Halp me!" It wasn't the front. It was coming from the back yard! I quickly opened the gate and ran as fast as I could to find Grandma on her knees, frozen, clinging to the trunk of a tree with her pants half down saying, "HALP ME!" My eyes scanned the yard to put the puzzle pieces together and my initial reaction was one of foul play but after further deduction, I figured it out. The shed, or 'garden house' door; as Grandma called it, was wide open and footprints in the snow led to an area where she wiped out, dropping the snow shovel. She then dragged herself halfway across the yard to a tree, slowly losing her pants on the way. Grandma made attempts to pick herself up out of the snow but got stuck on her knees with no hat or gloves; just a thin jacket that was wide open. Who knows how long she had been out there. It looked like hours! I freaked out and yelled for my girlfriend to open the back door as I ran to Grandma and embraced her.

"Everything's gonna be alright Grandma. I'm here!" My girlfriend approached the yard and asked what was going on. I was SO angry, words cannot express my feelings! The only thing I could say without being too nasty was, "This is what happens when I don't come right home from work! I hope you're happy! Now open the god damn back door!" She looked at Grandma, cried and went to unlock the house. I didn't care that I raised my voice and sounded mean. There was a part of me that was pleased to make her feel terrible for being selfish and demanding. I thought, "Maybe now she fuckin' gets it!" My point was made, but at Grandma's expense and I couldn't forgive this.

It is said that people are capable of great physical strength in times of disaster, especially when a loved one is in harm's way. I found this to be true as I wrapped my arms around her from behind in a bear hug and told her we were going to get her on her feet. She was so cold and mumbled, "I can't."

"I'm going to help you," as I lifted her dead weight to straighten out her legs. "OK. Now lean on me for a second," as I pulled her pants up as much as I could. Then I asked her to move her legs as I held on tight.

"I can't! I can't," she chattered.

"Yes, you can Grandma. I have you! You're not going to fall. I'm getting you to the warm house." I spooned her legs with mine and slowly nudged forward. She responded, agonizing from the pain of frostbite, but I urged her to continue as most of her weight was in my arms. "I have you! We're almost there! Just three steps up to the porch and we're in!"

My girlfriend opened the door for us and I instructed her to pull a kitchen chair to the middle of the room. Grandma's teeth chattered uncontrollably as I peeled the soaking wet clothes off her frozen skin. She kept repeating, "I'm not gonna make it. I'm not gonna make it." My girlfriend started crying again and I told her to go downstairs and stay there. I dashed to the linen closet and got a blanket to cover Grandma while filling a large pot with lukewarm water to soak and thaw her blue feet. Her feeble voice echoed itself, "I'm not gonna make it," as I vigorously rubbed her arms, back, and legs to warm her.

"If you're not gonna make it, then I'm going to have to call an ambulance," I loudly stated to snap her out of shock. "Do you want me to call an ambulance?" And I wondered if I should; she was frozen to the bone.

"No. No ambolinz," and she began to calm down. I checked her submerged feet and the color was returning so I fetched some dry clothes, toweled her off, and dressed her. Still shivering, I guided her into the living room, turned on the TV and lay with her on the couch under a blanket, spooning her to share my body heat. I held her hand and cuddled her for a couple of hours and Grandma finally thawed out. "Tank you Silvyaa," she said with warm relief and I replied, "I love you Grandma. Come on. Let's go tuck you in bed for the night." She concurred.

So many scenarios ran through my head that night. Grandma needed twenty-four-hour supervision. I thought about my old job in a nursing home when I was eighteen and couldn't bear the thought of Grandma being in there, so I would try as hard as I could to avoid it. The only way to do this would be to quit my job and get a part-time nurse to help occasionally. Plans were in the works to close the beauty salon which meant Grandma would be home indefinitely. I called my uncle with an update along with my idea. I was annoyed when he said it was too expensive to hire a visiting nurse. To try and prolong the inevitable, I did some research and found a senior center that could be used as a sort of babysitter while I worked during the day. It was a little pricey, so Grandma only went two or three times a week, but it was better than nothing!

It was difficult to convince Grandma to climb aboard the transportation van when it arrived the first few times. In the beginning, she was consumed with work and confused as to why the beauty shop was closed. She NEEDED to work, so I tried to get her to think that this was a career change, "Now you have a different job to go to during the week." This actually worked, and it got her in the van. If only we could just hire someone for those other couple of days or better yet, have my uncle watch her while I was at work. This would allow Grandma to maintain her freedom. Again, I ran the options by my uncle. He didn't go for it. It wasn't until he dropped by the house while I was working and found that Grandma had another misfire in the bathroom that he became motivated.

When I arrived home, he began screaming at me, "There's SHIT all over the bathroom! How could you leave it like THAT! It took me a LONG time to clean that mess UP!" I just stared at him until he was finished and then gave him a piece of my mind. "I have been doing this every day for over two years! You've got a lot of nerve! You are the one who has not been present and I see why!"

He didn't want to deal with this. He had no patience for her or any understanding of me. He didn't care for my honesty and accused me of being a freeloader; just hanging around for no other reason but to take advantage of Grandma. He immediately made arrangements with a nursing home, close to his residence, and made plans to liquidate her house and possessions as quickly as possible. I asked about buying the house, but he was not hearing anything I had to say. All at once, he took control and excluded me from everything. Many people told me he was a jerk, but I didn't believe it until this happened. I wondered why he was so bitter. I wondered if he remembered that Grandma and Grandpa raised me and they were essentially my parents too, whom I loved dearly. Was he angry that they took loving care of me? He did not share these same, kind parents, but that wasn't my fault! I was disgusted.

A date was set for Grandma Zofie's transition and I had a couple of months left with her at home. She was so angry with her son and complained that he was trying to put her away. "He's gonna clean me out!" I attempted to reassure her and change the subject, hoping she'd forget about it, but she didn't. I took her out to dinner as much as possible. She loved that. We kept trying Bingo, but it was becoming too confusing for her so we watched a lot of movies and visited her sisters often.

In the meantime, I needed to think about where I was going to live. I decided I wanted my own house and got pre-approved for a loan. I wasn't eligible for much money but found a cheap fixer-upper. It had a lot of character and potential, unlike some of the other dumps that were in my thirty-five-thousand-dollar price range. The day I closed on the house and got the keys, I had to call on a friend to help me repair major structural problems before even thinking about packing and moving. There was only a month left with Grandma and this would not be enough time, since I had to do most of the renovations on my own. The work was daunting, and I counted on a couple of extra weeks after Grandma's relocation to finish the huge job.

I drove Grandma over to see the progress on my new place and she didn't understand why I bought it, "You have a home!" With a tear in my eye, I responded, "I need to make arrangements for myself because I won't be allowed to stay at your house much longer." Grandma's brilliant blue eyes flashed as she sharply responded, "SAYS WHO?" I recounted the conversation my uncle and I had about the house and Grandma went on a verbal rant for the rest of the evening.

I was distraught over the whole ordeal, yet there was personal satisfaction to do this house thing completely on my own. I never imagined this would be attainable for me and I reflected on my life and gave thanks for surviving all I had gone through. I did not predict the possibilities of my present moment when I tried to interpret the "why's" of the past, but it did seem to be on purpose. It took time to see that all that stuff shaped me into who I was, and now, I was finally starting to like who I saw in the mirror. I could feel myself evolving and finally understood that the darkest hours of life are times of growth, if I allow them to be.

My last week with Grandma in the house I grew up in was sad and unsettling. I tried not to show it around her, even though I was falling apart. I was so attached to her, to this house and to so many memories. To make matters worse, my uncle acted surprised when he heard about my new house and said to me on the phone, "I wish you would've said something. I would've given you a sweet deal on this one!" I thought to myself, "Did he just say that?". It was too late! I couldn't find any words because I was choking on bullshit and buried in misunderstanding. "Well, if there's anything you need, just let me know and it's yours," he finished.

"Thanks. I'll keep that in mind," I hung up the phone and cried. Grandma asked me what was wrong and I told her I was having a bad day. We sat and watched TV as I smoked a few too many cigarettes, trying to relax. "When are you gonna quit doze cigrets? Dare no good for you!"

"Soon Grandma."

She squinted at me and knew I was lying, "Promise me you'll quit!"

"Ok Grandma, I promise." I had never broken a promise to her so far, but I wasn't sure I could keep this one.

Grandma kept talking about being sent away. I felt so bad for her and nothing I said could ease the pain. Sitting on the couch with tears rolling down her face, she said, "When I'm dead, I doan wanna be forgotten."

Empathetic, I stared at her and said, "You will NEVER be forgotten! And just because we're moving doesn't mean you won't see me anyone anymore. You're not being thrown out to the garbage!" I sobbed and hugged her tightly.

The next morning, we had coffee together and Grandma gave me the two rings on her finger that she always wore. When I was a kid, she told me that I was in her will and that someday I would have all her jewelry. I dreaded that day because it meant losing her. As a little girl, I used to cry myself to sleep, envisioning her death, wake, and funeral. Every night, I prayed to God to keep Grandma safe and never take her away from me. I even tried bargaining with the Almighty and said I would do anything for Grandma Zofie. Now, twenty-some years later, she was giving me what she cherished most. I told her I would lock them in a safe and reminded her that she wasn't dying, just moving. I forced myself to recall Grandma's wipe-outs onto the floor and consistent accidents to reassure myself that my uncle's tough decision about a nursing home was the right thing.

Only a couple more days were left and I didn't want the thought of it to wreck our day. It was Easter Sunday and we were going to dinner at my aunt and uncle's house for one last family gathering. I helped Grandma find something to wear and set it aside. She loved baths and I drew one for her many times, but after she got stuck and was unable to get herself out, we started using a shower chair. She never cared for a shower and, like a little kid, tried to avoid a clean-up. After a few minutes of convincing, I got her in there to scrub and rinse her thoroughly but quickly so she wouldn't get too cold from the air. I was savvy with making things easy for her and I know she appreciated it. Grandma was unstable on her feet and it was tough for her to get dressed sometimes, so we used the shower chair to assist us. After drying her off, we clothed the top half of her as she sat comfortably. This also made it easier to slip her bottoms on, up past her knees. When she stood to get out of the tub, she held on to me while I pulled her pants all the way up. Out of the bath we went, dressed and ready for hair and makeup!

I wanted to make Grandma's hair beautiful and every time I worked on it I was nervous. Being in the business all her life, she kept it perfect and I wasn't skilled enough to give her a proper 'up-do', as she called it.

"I can't do it as good as you, Grandma!"

She smiled and said, "Dats Ok, juss put a couple curls here and dare."

I did the best I could and enjoyed seeing Grandma relax as I played with her hair. She told me that if I went to cosmetology school, she'd give me the beauty salon and I could take over. I was also cutting hair at that time but it was pet grooming. I definitely preferred animals over people and hoped that my refusal of Grandma's offer didn't disappoint her.

All set and ready for dinner, we got in the car and I took my time, pointing out some of the beautiful landscape on the way for us to enjoy together. Again, she complimented my driving and said I would be a good race car driver. Maybe it was the way I passed people or changed lanes or something. I'm not sure. Being a race car driver was one of her dreams that she claimed Grandpa held her back from pursuing. In the time of her youth, it wasn't a woman's 'place' to do such a thing, but she wanted to do it anyways. Her eyes would sparkle every time she mentioned it. This desire manifested itself a few times in the form of speeding tickets. The judge in court took one look at her, smiled and said, "At your age, you are exempt from school. Just try to slow down and don't do 55mph around corners." I must admit, it was cute seeing my eighty-something year old grandmother claiming her innocence to a judge!

Grandma and I had a nice dinner at my uncle's, and boy, my aunt sure had Grandma's recipes down pat. The food was delicious! I picked up a vibe at the table and could tell that my relatives were experiencing a similar sadness of this being 'the last supper'. We were able to visit for a couple of hours before Grandma had an accident. There is a saying when you get old …never trust a fart. This is so true! I took Grandma home, cleaned her up and then we watched TV together before turning in for the night. This was the last time she would sleep in her own bed and I thought about when I used to sleep next to her when I was under her care as a little girl. Tonight, I would do the same and listen to her cute little snores as I lay awake watching the shadows in the room, just like old times.

In the morning, I opened my eyes to see her sleeping peacefully. Careful not to disturb her, I lay on my side and watched until she awoke, amused as the morning light put her into a hypnotic stare that drew her gaze to the window.

"Good morning Grandma."

Her eyes moved to greet mine, smiling, "Ga mornin."

My mind flashed back to when she would tickle my feet to get me out of bed for breakfast, "I'll go make us some coffee before I take off for work." There was a part of me that was glad to go. Today was Grandma's big day. My aunt and uncle were coming later to take her to the nursing home and I couldn't handle seeing that. I knew she would put up a fight …A BIG one! For now, she had forgotten and we were having a nice morning. I chose this peaceful interaction to be my last memory of us in this house together. I tried my best not to be bummed out, especially when I asked her what was wrong as she sat on the couch and stared out the window. "I'm just waiting to die," she said. I gave her a big kiss and a hug before I left for work.

At the grooming shop, I was distracted the entire day and when I came home to a quiet house, I walked around from room to room, weeping. I already missed her and was worried for her. That evening, the phone rang and it was my uncle. I asked how it went today and he said it was horrible. Grandma didn't understand and thought she was being left behind, dumped off, and forgotten. She got nasty with him and I could picture it in my head. For a moment, I had compassion until he abruptly said, "Where are Grandma's rings? I noticed that she didn't have them on at dinner yesterday."

"She gave them to me Easter morning."

"Bullshit! She's not even dead yet and you're taking her rings! You've got a lot of nerve you son of a bitch!"

"How dare you! Grandma's been telling me ever since I was little that I would have her jewelry someday. She gave them to me and I'm glad. I'm sure they would have disappeared in the nursing home and she knew that."

"I want those rings back!" Click! He hung up on me. He had it in his head that EVERYTHING belonged to him. He put the house on the market and kicked me out as quickly as he could to have an estate sale and be rid of everything. Earlier in the week, he told me to take anything

I needed for my new house. The only thing I asked for was the old washer and dryer and his response was, "Well . . . I don't know. I'm not sure what I'm going to do. I'm going to hold on to that for now." I reminded him of our prior conversation and then realized that he had no intentions of giving me anything at all. He continued to harass me about Grandma's rings and gave me a week to get out of the house. The endless pestering was so bad, to the point that it wasn't worth the aggravation, so I gave him the rings along with a few honest words about "doing what was right". I enlightened him on how I was warned by numerous people that he would keep my mother's share of everything when the time came. These words must've shocked him and struck a chord because a couple days later, he offered me Grandma's dining room set. I declined, but did accept the couch. I was extremely bitter and grabbed a couple more pieces of furniture on my way out, knowing that everything of sentimental value would be sold. Grandpa Loosha had many cases of his homemade wine left. I'm glad I took a few boxes because the guy who bought the wine press also took the rest of the irreplaceable wine. I moved out in a hurry to my unfinished house at my uncle's insistence and planned on writing him off. To my surprise, after a few months of bumping into him at the nursing home, he returned Grandma's rings to me. I wondered if he read the will and discovered that I wasn't a thief. I decided to try and forgive him.

In the beginning, visiting Grandma was challenging. She had dementia but wasn't completely out of her mind and the nurses got to know me by name very quickly as Grandma asked for me all day long. Every time I went to visit, she thought I was there to pick her up and take her home. She looked thrilled to see me and desperate to leave, but when I reminded her that the house was sold, she got mad and felt stranded. I wanted to take her to my new house and care for her. If only I could afford to quit the new job I started. Sometimes she would literally beg me to get her out of there and I had to lie and tell her I was on my way to work and would return later. My aunt and uncle were experiencing similar traumatic visits. Every time I left her there, I cried so hard that I had to sit in my car for twenty minutes to compose myself to be able to drive.

As Grandma's mind and mobility declined, she stopped asking about home. I fed her lunch sometimes, took her for wheelchair rides outside on warm days, and watched TV with her in her room. She still had her sense of humor and laughed at the comedy shows. I recall one particular skit on a 'funny videos' show, when a bald broadcaster telling a serious story in the news had a huge fly buzz around and land on his head. Grandma's whole body jiggled with laughter and it was times like these that made me feel better. On occasion, she would reminisce and then tell me that I should follow my dreams. When I asked how I should go about doing that, she told me, "Pay attention to watt you're NOT doing! Furgit about yer monkey business and stop wastin' time." I understood what she meant. I was easily distracted from listening to anything my inner self wished to do. There was always an excuse as to why I didn't follow my heart. I was too busy, too afraid of failure or disappointment if things didn't work out the way I wanted them to. I assumed there was too much difficulty in making dreams a reality. I questioned my purpose while going about daily mundane routines; feeling as though something was missing. I would contemplate Grandma's words and continually try to improve my awareness and my life in general.

Grandma Zofie lived in the nursing home for three years before her death in late October of 2002. The day I had dreaded all my life was here and I was now seeing with my own eyes the same images I had visualized as a little girl. I never thought she would be the first of her sisters to go. Thankfully, one of them blessed me with some comic relief at the wake. Carol, the oldest sister, who was well into her nineties, was stricken with dementia and didn't know who was in the casket. Auntie Carol's kids were embarrassed as she approached, looked in and said, "I doan no who dat is!" Yet, she insisted on staying for a moment to say a prayer for the dead. I smiled at my cousins and said I understood and they looked at me a bit cross when I started to laugh. When Aunt Carol made it to her seat, I chatted with her, "How are you Auntie? It's good to see you!"

Breathing a little heavy, she said, "It's good to see you too! Now who are you again?"

"I'm Sylvia."

"Oh yeahhhh …Silvyaa! How are you?"

"I'm good. How are you? You look great Auntie Carol!"

"Tank you. I feel about as good as dat one in da box over dare!" We both cracked up laughing! I was thankful for her lightheartedness and it was just what I needed. I was glad for our encounter and annoyed with the family when she died a short time later and I was not told.

Many of my friends came to pay their respects because they all understood how important Grandma was to me. After the funeral, I went home and fell to my knees at the side of my bed and sobbed for at least an hour straight. I was paralyzed in prayer position and cried so hard, my nose started to bleed all over my bed, face, and hands. At that moment, a burst of sunlight shone through the clouds and touched me as I knelt. I lifted myself up and walked across the hallway to the window, crying and bleeding, feeling more vacant than I had ever felt. I stared into the sun as I whimpered, looking for Grandma. Its strength grew so bright I had to close my eyes as the warmth on my face calmed me down. "Grandma? I love you so much Grandma," as I sniffled, shook, and used all of my might to smile back at the sun. For an unforgettable and peaceful moment, all my hopelessness disappeared. With that, the clouds slowly blanketed the sun and gently put it to sleep. "Thank you." I whispered and then walked to the bathroom to wash my face.

Reflection: From that moment on, I adopted a completely different view about death. I had seen so much of it and most of my immediate family was gone. At times, I felt orphaned, completely alone, uncertain of my own fate, and wondered if I would die early on in life to join all of them. I searched myself for a sense of purpose, but could not see any. I didn't know how long I could walk blindly through life. Thinking about and missing my family gave me a sense of longing to be with them and I didn't really care if I died. I would think about them and occasionally get a sense that they were with me, watching, comforting, and cheering me on. At first, I didn't know if this was my imagination or not, but it gave me the strength to say to myself, "Everything is OK. Everything is as it should be. Keep going."

Rather than being devastated and melancholy over the news of someone's death, I found a certain, "Good for you. You Graduated," frame of mind. I discovered that it was my own selfishness that brought about lingering dismal moods and now knew it was possible to carry on with their strength and wisdom by my side, even though I could no longer physically see them.

CHAPTER 8

SPRING RAIN

OVER THE NEXT SIX years, I immersed myself in a lot of books based on spirituality, meditation, and self-help. Some were good reads and others not so much, but there were interesting concepts in all of them that I took into consideration and used as guidance. I focused on writing, performing as a singing drummer and meditating frequently. At the time, I was asking myself a lot of questions like, "Why am I unable to maintain a good and loving relationship with someone?" I lost myself in a daydream and zoned in on the poor examples my mother gave. I thought about Grandma Zofie and Grandpa Loosha cohabitating with constant bickering and separate bedrooms. I wondered if I was inherently dysfunctional in some way. Though I was surrounded by bad examples, I had a picture in my mind, attached with strong conviction, of what a healthy relationship should be. It would be loving and thoughtful, respectful and fun, intimate and safe with open communication. It would include REASONABLE compromise, of course. Sounds good, right? Sounds like the basic principles that everyone deserves to enjoy. I concluded that I was looking too much at the outside of a person rather than focusing on what was inside. I had put a lot of stock into being physically attracted to someone as the 'green light' to emotionally involve myself and invest in a relationship. I reasoned that perhaps I was shallow and wasn't giving the 'right person' even a glimpse, so I observed other people and tried to understand why the nerdy, unattractive guy had the hot girl. Why was the no-tooth, abrasive woman at the bar hooked up? It didn't seem fair. What was in MY way?

In search of happiness, I sold the stock I had in being with my 'ideal type' and settled into an average, long-term relationship with someone talented, creative, and loyal. At first, this was a nice change and we fared well. As time passed, the red flags started waving and I realized that I was living with a grumpy woman. Even with compromise, I found myself trapped in negativity and in a spiritual dead-zone of sorts. I sought the advice of friends and they shared their stories with me about the ups and downs of their marriages, yet they remained together. So, I decided to ignore the colorlessness of my cohabitation with my partner and just went along with it, even though I wasn't happy. Because this was not in alignment with my spirit, I grew irritable and couldn't stand myself. I rarely engaged in my spiritual practices and finally had to muster up the courage to listen to my inner voice and leave the relationship. My decision was not well received, but after being separated, she realized that it was the right thing to do for both of us. It was time to focus on me!

I moved on and bought a new house, ironically enough, across the street from the grammar school where I met some of the most important people in my life. Things were coming full circle and now, at the age of thirty-nine, I felt like I was finally evolving. On occasion, a painful melancholy revisited, and ghosts of the past revealed themselves, but I was able to put things into better perspective. I began to interpret these emotions as a strength within myself to overcome obstacles. Sometimes I forgot this and got tripped up, which led to days of walking blindly again, wondering what the hell happened to my good vibes and clear head. Upon further examination, I noticed that fear and doubt were two of the most debilitating mind games I played on myself. It was only when I continually reminded myself to stick with positivity that things eventually worked out.

I have heard people say (and I have said it as well), "I feel like I'm going out of my mind!" The real issue is that we are "IN our minds" too much! The mind is always busy building scenarios and jumping from one worry to the next rather than allowing the quiet pauses in between to calm us down and make room for peace. After many fruitless searches, I've learned that the answers in life are accessible to me below all the brain chatter. There is a wise being living inside of me. This is the divine. This is connection to the one who has always been right, strong, and constant. This is where my gut feelings come from to help make wise decisions. This is my true self and where love can be found. This is where everything is found!

It has been a challenge to quiet my mind and listen to the silence that resides there. It seems that these brief moments of peace are too few and far between and have left me feeling defeated. Yet, I believe it's important to not give up. Instead, I cut myself a break and continue to pursue being a better listener for longer periods of time. The proof shows itself when the "busy mind" is back in business and I have a better ability to manage daily stress, to let go of the negative and insignificant events of the day, and focus more on how to allow for happiness in the present moment. I made it a personal goal to tame my mind and not be "that person" (and we all know of at least one), who is completely unaware of how annoying they are with constant chattering complaints.

I also focused my attention on self-healing and, for me, it started with the art of forgiveness. The results yielded incredible benefits as I allowed this release of negative energy. I have forgiven my stepfather for the damage he caused. This has led to deep and healing conversations with him. In the far future, I would care for him as he was dying. If someone told me when I was younger that I would do the things I did for him, I would never have believed it. I have forgiven my mother and father for leaving me with abandonment and trust issues. This has led to a deep understanding of myself. Finding compassion, I forgave the men in my life that used me, and I am no longer burdened with animosity. I forgave my parents' siblings for selfishly taking my share of everything after my grandparents' passing. This sparked major inner discord and I was poisoned with judgement. This was difficult to let go of, and I gave audience to it for far too long because I couldn't ignore my mind telling me that life had been unfair. This resulted in resentment and I'm just plain tired of that path! I do my best to be mindful of my emotions when they stir and, with practice, it's getting easier. On the other hand, learning to forgive myself for any hurt that I may have projected onto other people has been a battle.

Wouldn't it be nice if we could prevent our own mistakes by paying attention to the outcome of the actions of others? So much time and energy could be saved, but I guess maybe life would be boring if that were the case. I condemned myself to endless punishment when I didn't have the opportunity to make things right with the faults of my past. People moved on and disappeared. Many times, I didn't have the opportunity to say, "I'm sorry" to someone who deserved an apology.

My beloved Grandma Zofie was one of those people. One morning, late for work, the mental stress of coping with her dementia showed itself as I bundled her up and walked her to my vehicle. I don't even remember what set me off, but what I can't forget is when I clenched her shoulders, shook her and yelled in her face, "Are you having a bad day?" She cowered and nodded a "yes" as I stared into her confused blue eyes. The inner horror and guilt I experienced IMMEDIATELY (like when a cute little furry creature gets caught up in the spinning car wheel), brought me to tears and still bothers me to this day. Self-forgiveness has been challenging, and it took time and re-evaluation to adjust how I thought about myself. For so many years, I focused on all of the bad things that happened, poor choices I'd made, and the overall hurt and emptiness I felt. It was difficult to bring to the forefront of my mind anything good. My mind is very stubborn and I spent a lot of time forcing myself to think about anything I did to help someone, even if it was as simple as a few nice words. Sometimes, I would turn off the phone, TV, radio, whatever created a distraction, and sit on in my rocking chair and just stare into space. My intention was to visualize and relive the moments that held a good feeling. After trying this a few times, not giving in to the frustration of not being able to focus very well, I rediscovered fond memories from long ago that

I hadn't thought about since the day they happened. A number of times, I fell into laughing fits while remembering some of the wild things my friends and I did together. This led to my thoughts diving deeper to times when friends were at the end of their rope and desperately sought out my counsel. Geez! I never took into consideration the trust and admiration a person must've had for me, to be considered their crisis "go to" person. I began to see myself in a different light. My perspective was altered and loved myself just a little more. My attitude changed and allowed healing to pour in. I realized that pain and suffering was an important part of the human experience …a teacher at my side to remind me of what my character was built on.

It was exciting to find more healing and closure with a fresh, positive attitude. I thought about the years when I felt victimized and the fact is: I truly was. I had no control over most of the events of my young life. Those scars carried over into adulthood and, for a long time, I believed that I was entitled to something. During this time, I couldn't see the forest through the trees. I didn't realize, as the negativity was running rampant in my life and mind, that I was receiving the best deal EVER! All the past prepared me for NOW and the Now had become quite interesting. What I thought was impossible, now, was not. The unfinished business …the times that made me feel alone and invisible to the world …the empty street that always led me back to the past, no longer led anywhere important. I finally realized that there is no life there. There is only the NOW.

So, with that I spent the next summer enjoying a new-found freedom as I meditated on the powers of self-healing. It was like feeling the wind blowing through my hair for the first time and breathing in precious clean air that for so long had been stagnant. I was on my own, basking in the quiet of my dwelling, never feeling alone. I knew for sure that the powers of the universe were vast beyond comprehension and always watched over me, providing just what I needed.

I made plans to drive across the country to escort my friend Sarah, a traveling nurse and former band mate, to her new assignment in Arizona. I'd always dreamed of doing such a thing. So, what better time than now! I was adventurous in spirit, for one. I also wanted a healing experience in the desert. It was as if I would relive some of what my mom had experienced when she left me to go on the road when I was a baby.

As I anticipated my trip over the next few months, my leisure time was spent on the social circuit meeting a lot of fun and interesting people, mostly through Sarah. She and I were making up for lost time and hung out constantly. It seemed so long ago that we were in a band together ripping up the town and it was good to be around someone fun, interesting, and a little crazy. It was inspiring, and I was prompted to live again! Sarah was a free spirit that liked to fly, and I thought, "Aren't we all?" I contemplated this for a long while one evening while swaying in my favorite rocking chair, where I've always done my best thinking, praying, and problem solving. I asked the 'powers that be' for guidance as I pondered where I was going and what I was supposed to do in this world. My head seemed to be in the right place and yet I felt a hole in my life . . . a familiar inner plaguing that seemed unshakeable. I wished to be free of it and asked for clarity and healing before I went to sleep.

The work week drew to a close and it was Friday night. With a deep sigh of relief, I slipped on my comfy sweats and T-shirt, "AH! I can sleep in tomorrow!" I usually retired early with a book as the cats joined me and competed for my attention by standing on my lap, blocking my view of a good read. I never answered my phone once I settled in, but tonight was different. Someone left two messages and for some reason, I became as curious as the cats. Both calls came from the same number and it seemed urgent, so I returned the call to find my old high-school buddy on the line. The low voice said, "Sylvia man, Jess is here."

I rolled my eyes, "AND?"

She knew my past with Jess, "Why don't you come out to the bar I'm working at?"

"I'm already in bed."

"AT THIS EARLY HOUR?" She laughed as she spoke to someone else, "I told you she'd be in bed already! Come out Sylvia. Get dressed and come here."

I fought with my inconvenience, "How long is she staying?"

Again, the low voice, "I'll get her to stay. Just get moving!"

A long hesitation and then, "Alright. I'll be there shortly."

I hung up the phone and hurried to find something casual to wear. I was excited, nervous, cautious and cynical all at once and with good reason. This girl was the ghost that haunted me for the past twenty-three years. My mind raced during the entire car ride. I didn't know what to expect so I tried not to expect anything, good or bad. When I arrived, and stepped through the door, there she was, sitting at the end of the bar. I glanced at my buddy with eyebrows raised and walked over to Jess and pulled up a chair, "Long time no see."

Jess seemed happy to see me and we chatted for a while about what we've both been up to over the years. As we talked about her nine-year old son, a big creepy looking dude with some missing teeth and fuzzy hair came over and kissed her cheek. My stomach churned and I woke up from the dreamy state I had fallen into. When he went to take his shot at the pool table, Jess told me he was just a friend that called on the fly to just hang out and get out of the house for a while. "I didn't really want to hang with him, but I was bored," she stated uncomfortably. I didn't trust this, but offered her a ride home if she really didn't want to be around him. She was enjoying a good beer buzz and her face expressed indecision, so I just left the offer on the table and let it go.

Jess excused herself to go to the lady's room and Mr. Creepy slithered over, put his hand on my leg and started talking. I gently removed his paw and told him to keep it to himself. He made small talk and mentioned that he was leaving soon to go make a few thousand bucks selling cocaine. I told him I would give Jess a ride. With that, she reappeared from the restroom and they discussed how she was getting home. He shot her a perverted look and nodded to me, indicating that if she wanted a woman tonight, here's her chance. The thought did cross my mind at one point but the nausea put an end to that quickly. I looked at her and said, "I'll drive, but it's up to you." I went to the restroom and when I returned a moment later, she was sitting in his car. I guess she made her choice. It would've been nice to get an answer from her rather than a disappearing act, but some things apparently don't change. I stood outside for a smoke and she looked up at me as he got into the driver's seat. We stared at each other for a moment. The look on my face must have revealed disappointment in her because she put her head down as if ashamed. When she looked back at me again, I motioned for her to call me sometime and she smiled as they drove off. I never expected to hear from her again.

Over the next couple of days, Sarah and I planned more of our cross-country road trip and decided to take old Route 66. How excited we both were! Some destinations were planned, like the Painted Desert, Sedona and the Grand Canyon, but we made it a point to be spontaneous and stop at any points of interest on the way. I loved spontaneity! I was full of questions about my life and direction but at least now, I was more open to whatever came my way. In that mindset, I received a phone call. It was Jess and I couldn't believe my ears. She apologized for the other night and wanted to get together. I invited her and her son to come to my home for a visit and she eagerly agreed.

When they arrived, I had butterflies in my belly. She looked great with a warm smile and her son seemed like a fun and interesting kid. He took to me rather quickly as most kids do. I have a lot of intriguing and fun stuff around the house that a kid would like: drums, guitars, X-Box, and junk food. They stayed for a while and the longer I was around her, the more I wanted to re-live our first kiss. As I watched them leave, there was a jolt in my heart that was both piercing and soothing. I still had love for her after so many years, even amidst the hurt and abandonment. I was certain. There was unfinished business here and I thanked the powers that be for bringing about this reunion and answering my request for clarity.

Jess and I started with texting frequently. She had a "wonderful time" during our visit and admitted she wanted to kiss me. I laughed and said I had the same thought. One evening, I decided I was going to use a sick day for work the next morning and, if she felt like joining me, we could hang out together. When she said she'd text me early in the morning to let me know, that morning couldn't come fast enough! I promptly called in and patiently waited. 6am. 7am. By 8am, my bubble was bursting and I assumed it was a 'no go'. Then my phone rang and her voice greeting me, "You haven't responded to any of my texts and I thought it unusual. Are we still on for today?"

Surprised, I said, "I haven't gotten any texts. I thought you were blowing me off." With further investigation, somehow there was a block on my phone to receive any texts from her. Was this a sign? Hmmm. We laughed about it and she came over to spend the late morning with me.

I opened the door to find Jess smiling and looking more beautiful than I had ever remembered. How I had missed her. We sat on the couch and made small talk as we studied each other intently. I moved closer and held her hand, thankful that she was here now, looking me in the eyes.

The magnetism was overpowering and we found each other's lips again after so long. It was magical! I ran my fingers through her long brown hair and traced the lines of her face to see if she was real. Her eyes were so dark and I found myself lost in them. We held one another and wished we had more time alone, but she had to leave to pick her son up from school. Before she left, we talked about how we wrote each other love letters but never signed our names and destroyed them in fear of being found out. I said, "It was difficult for me to rip up those letters after reading them." We both agreed that the timing was just bad. High school in the 1980's in our little town, was not the place to come out of the closet, or even admit to experimentation. We wanted to write letters to one another and, this time, we would sign and keep them. And so, we began again.

In October of 2008, I attended a civil union between a friend of mine and her girlfriend in a beautiful Japanese Garden. Unfortunately, gay marriage was not yet legal, but that time would finally arrive soon. The ceremony was absolutely beautiful, and the reception was a blast! I was so happy for them as I could see and feel the love between them. I thought about Jess and wondered if this would be us some day. The love I carried in my heart for this woman led me to believe that I was meant to spend the rest of my life with her. I gave her a call during the reception dinner and told her what a great time I was having. We wanted to see each other and so decided I would drop by afterwards. My thoughts were preoccupied for the remainder of the celebration.

I felt good. I looked good, being all dressed up for the wedding. Mostly, I felt excited to be knocking on her door. She greeted me with those eyes and a smile that shot a hot vibe through me. I was invited to sit with her on the love seat as her son hogged the entire couch. I didn't mind. She had a blanket to keep us cozy warm where we sat and held hands under covers. Her son didn't know yet that his mother and I were in love and had been for many years. We wondered what his nine-year-old thoughts were on gay people, if he had those thoughts at all. We hoped he would understand eventually that love is love no matter who. He was a very bright, observant little boy, wise beyond his years and surprised me with some of the 'adult like' topics he would later bring up. But for that moment, Jess and I decided to wait until the time was right. We watched TV and painted with some of his arts and crafts for a while. Jess asked if I would stay the night as she handed me my first new love letter. After reading it, there was nothing I wanted to do more.

Jess tucked her son in for the night, leaving the TV on for him in case he didn't fall asleep right away. She escorted me to her room and closed the door, lighting a candle so we could see each other and talk quietly. "I love you," we exchanged with a passionate kiss and made love that night for the first time in twenty-three years. It was surreal.

The next morning, she made breakfast and said that her son would be with his dad for the weekend. Jess was hoping to spend that free time with me. Of course, I said, "Yes!" Before I knew it, she was at my house and we did a lot of catching up. Later, we retired to my room and held one another listening to music, and I sang to her. In those moments, I saw a familiar look on her face. She turned cold, got up and went into the bathroom for what seemed a very long time. All of a sudden, I was flooded with horrible emotions from the past. She had done this to me before …hot and then completely cold, leading me on and then turning her back on me for no apparent reason. My eyes welled up when she returned and laid down next to me. I explained what was going on; I never understood her actions in the past and I could not go through that again.

Jess held me and started to cry. She confessed, "When you looked me in the eyes and sang sweetly to me, I was hit with a tidal wave of emotion." In that moment, she realized just how bad she hurt me. "In high school, you were such a bad-ass and always walked with confidence and seemed so strong. I thought you could handle anything! Watching you tonight made me see that you are a beautiful and sensitive girl. I had to get up and walk away from you because I feel so completely horrible for what I've done to you. My God …I'm so sorry! I'm so sorry!"

We held each other so tight, balling our eyes out as she continued with all the apologies I so badly needed to hear. Jess regretted the time lost between us and admitted to thinking about me often; calling my house throughout the years to hear my voice answer the phone before hanging up. One time, she took one of my band flyers off the wall at a bar and took it home with her and she went on to say that she wanted to spend the rest of her life doing everything possible to make me happy. "I love you with every ounce of my being. There will never be anyone but you!" As she spoke, I felt the entire weight of the world lift from my chest. All those years we had starved for love and the bottomless need for each other was finally brought into the light. It was dreamy, other worldly, and complete. We felt like we'd known each other for thousands of years. The love we made that night was so intense, "I need you more than air," she cried.

My road trip to Arizona was here and Jess flooded me with love letters before I departed. I was so happy! Jess was nervous though, and thought she would lose me to Sarah during the trip. I didn't understand the insecurity vibe and reassured her by promising to call frequently. I purchased matching Celtic eternity bands for us to wear and gave her my house key to go there any time in my absence.

The road trip was life altering! Spontaneous pit stops were loads of fun and the places I saw were breath taking. The first time I thought about my mother was when Sarah and I explored the Painted Desert. It was a very wakeful moment when we hiked through the Blue Mesa region. I felt like I was exploring another planet. The landscape was completely surreal and my mother's pictures that I sifted through as a child did not do it justice. My thought was, "She left me behind to see THIS! How can I be mad about that!" What I beheld left me in awe with tears in my eyes as I intermingled with Spirit, listening to the silence.

Another profound experience I had early on was at "Spider Rock" in Canyon de Chelly. There's an old Native American story passed down to the children about the divine spider woman who lives there and how she crawls down the rock and takes the bad children back up to eat them. The entire story is quite interesting if you want to google it. We went there early in the morning and the air was crispy cold with a fresh dusting of snow. I was pleased that we were the only ones there. It was so quiet and peaceful! As I gazed down upon Spider Rock, sitting majestically in the canyon, bathed by a light fog, a bird of prey flew above my head. I could hear perfectly as the wind rushed under her pumping wings. Every stoke …woosh …woosh …woosh …was absolutely magnificent! The energy was incredible, and I was inspired to shout into the canyon. "Hellooooo," and the echo went on and on for what I thought to be an amazingly long time. To my surprise, I was answered! Howl after howl echoed back to me from a huge pack of either dogs or wolves or both! I gasped as my eyes lit up and I stood at attention in silence, awe and complete gratitude. Wow! I thought about Jess and our draw to wolves and Native American culture.

I wondered if we shared a life here, in another time. I shouted her name into the Canyon before I left.

The next stop was the Grand Canyon and it was astonishing! We hiked, rode horses and drove around the rim to different areas all day to see as much as we could. The depth, the colors, the rock formations carved by Mother Nature were nothing less than perfect. By early evening, Sarah and I shared a bottle of wine and watched the sun set over the Canyon. It was total Rockstar!!! I was thankful for my friendship with Sarah and for this adventure. In the morning, we headed to Sedona and explored the mystical landscape and vortex areas. I was humbled by the beauty of this place, with its red rocks reaching for the deep blue sky, and sensed that a higher consciousness resided there. I knew in my heart that I must return and spend more time in this place.

I checked in with Jess and she was eager for me to come home. She cried on the phone and said she missed me terribly and spent the night at my house to feel closer to me. I was happy to know that she missed me, but it seemed her over reaction to my absence was a little odd. I missed her too, but certainly wasn't going to wish away my trip so that I could get home. I thought this to be a little red flag but I was so thankful for our reunion that backing off was not an option. Sometimes, people can't put the words to their feelings and music explains emotion so much better. When she told me to listen to a song called "Everything" from Lifehouse, she said it expressed how she felt for me. I know she was insecure about my being on a trip with a good friend and I promised to listen to it. When I settled in for the night and looked it up, I shook my head with a tear in my eye, looked to the heavens from Arizona and said, "Thank you!"

One of the last stops we made before heading home was to Flagstaff, Arizona. The most memorable thing for me was a pit-stop at a local spiritual store. The owner, from what I remember, was a chanting monk who now had a new life and was in business selling musical instruments from around the world along with spiritual trinkets, incense and the like. He turned me on to an instrument called a Monochord and as I reclined on a "sound bed", he played and chanted for me. The experience was so moving that I considered buying this thing and shipping it home until I found out that it was thousands of dollars. Maybe next time. I imagined having this beautiful piece in my home some day and now had a new-found interest in Sound Healing. I'm sure that my musical background intensified this 'draw' and I felt the need to explore this healing modality further when I returned home. When Sarah dropped me off at the Phoenix airport, we said our temporary goodbyes, knowing we would travel together again soon. Now, it was time to get back home and start a new life with my girl.

Jess greeted me at the airport as I stepped out of the gate. Looking at her made me feel glad to be home. I thought to myself, "All those years of torment can now be laid to rest. I have been given the opportunity to live out my dreams with her. Thank you!" She carried one of my bags for me and as we walked to the car, she told me, "I was so nervous and worked up that when I watched you walk through security and look for me, I almost blacked out." The whole ride home, we held hands, looked at each other and couldn't stop smiling. I was convinced that we were meant to be. So, for the next few weeks, we spent lots of time together. Her son grew attached to me and kept saying how happy his mother was when she was around me. Jess and I decided, it was time to let him know about us. We were worried about his response and it was especially important to me, based on my past experience with judgement, that he be accepting. He was thrilled about it and wanted us all to be together! We were ecstatic! This little boy witnessed people floating in and out of his mother's life, including his father, that brought nothing but chaos. He needed stability. Jess did too, and this was something I could provide; I wanted to provide. I wanted to fix everything for them and knew that I could.

Telling Jess's mom, on the other hand, sparked a lot of uneasiness and we tried to figure out the best way to do it. When Jess and I hung out together in High School, her mother sensed that I was gay and had a BIG problem with it. The fear instilled in Jess was incredibly difficult for her to deal with which led to being afraid of labels, opinions and judgements of others. This paved the way to becoming a very private and withdrawn person. If the spot-light was pointed at her, she automatically denied anything and ran for cover. Being in a same-sex relationship would be a huge hurdle for her to jump, but she was now willing to face it. Jess slowly brought my name up in conversations with her mother, mentioning that we were hanging out. Her response was usually, "Why?" Or, "What are you doing hanging around with HER?" Jess and I joked about it and were not surprised by the reaction, but hoped that she would come around. She would HAVE TO eventually because we planned on moving in together.

For a rational mind, it seemed a little too fast to plan such a thing. Jess and I conversed, agreed that too much time had already been lost between us, and concluded that it was the right thing to do for us and for her son. We felt blessed to be given another chance and, again, that it was meant to be. I did have to address a strong concern in my mind, though, before committing completely. Because of the past, there still remained a deep wound. I questioned her numerous times about her true feelings and sexuality, "Jess, I am a full-blown lesbian. There is NO in-between. This is how I am. I'm comfortable in my own skin and don't care about the opinions of others. I don't want to dwell on the past and hold any distrust in you as we move forward. I have always loved you and want to share my life with you, but you must be ABSOLUTELY SURE because I would not be able to handle the heartbreak if you turned your back on me again. It has taken me years of distraction and contemplation to heal and get you out of my head. I will not be that jealous and angry person, having to compete with men in your life. I can't go through that again."

Her reassurance was convincing, "You are the love of my life! I love the fact that we don't have to hide what we feel for each other anymore. I want to scream to the world how much I care for you and with every moment we spend together, my love grows stronger still." She continued, almost poetically, "You have every ounce of my love, my being, my soul. This is one of a kind. You are my purpose. You give me peace. How could I have ever lived so long without you? I've prayed and prayed and now you're with me. There won't be any bullshit or sadness. I look forward to growing with you, helping each other, and feeling complete. With you in my life, there will be nothing we can't deal with. Our souls belong together and you are truly a blessing! I love you baby!"

Well, on that note! OK! These are only a few of the things she said in her letters. I thought I was dreaming. Jess expressed the reassurance I needed to hear which filled me with gratitude and thought it to be a miracle sent from God. She came back. All those things she said in High School were not lies, just bad timing. Now we were free to fly with one another!

Jess packed up her home and moved in with me. Both she and her son seemed excited to declutter and ready themselves for a new beginning. He would have his own room and start at a new school, escaping the bullying he was experiencing. I sensed that Jess was a little stressed at first. All her things were scattered and in boxes, so I told her to take liberties to rearrange the house and incorporate her things into the décor. I wanted her to know that this was not only MY house, but HERS as well. Everything I owned was for us to share and hoped that she would feel like it was "home". She told me she really liked the way I had things in the house and didn't want to change anything. This concerned me, and I took it upon myself to hang a few of her things, hoping she'd get the message. I wanted her to be completely comfortable. She and her son would now be safe and secure. We would work together and raise her child as a family. It seemed perfect.

Once settled, Jess told her mom that she had moved in with me. Her initial response was, "What will you do after a couple of months when she doesn't want you there anymore?" I was a little hurt by that, knowing I would not turn my back on Jess. I hoped and prayed her mother could somehow understand how much I truly loved her daughter. I wanted her to like me and it seemed important that our relationship be accepted by her. I wasn't that smart-ass sixteen-year-old any more that didn't seem to have a bright future. Her daughter was with one of the best people around: a person that would care for her, love, help and support her. Damn it! Just BE THERE for her! Didn't she want to see Jess happy? Soon, she would notice positive changes in her daughter and grandson.

The first challenge was getting some consistency for her son. Laying down some basic house rules like bed time and cleaning up after himself proved to be challenging. Jess had catered to his every whim, so introducing a little personal responsibility and schedules were of course, resisted. She and I discussed some things and she started to realize the importance of providing him a solid foundation on which to grow. He was a smart kid and I talked with him and explained how these things would help him. Sometimes he understood and other times he didn't but we were going to work through it. Change wasn't going to happen overnight.

My little buddy was excited about starting a new school at first and hoped to make friends. He tended to have a hard time with this and I felt bad for him. Kids, especially pre-teens, can be extremely nasty and he discovered this quickly. It also didn't help that he had ADHD. In general, he was very disorganized, forgetful and sensitive. When kids were mean to him at school, he didn't understand why. He simply wanted was a friend. And so, he began acting up at school. Then he would come home and pitch a fit about doing his homework, eating dinner at the table, and going to bed at the designated time. The disrespect at home and at school needed to be handled. Jess saw this and felt she was a bad mother that hadn't been present for him throughout his childhood by ignoring issues and not setting a good example. She was now full of regrets, wishing she had taught him better. I reassured her that given her past situations, she had done the best she could all by herself, and that it was not too late to point him in the right direction. He liked books, loved drawing and I noticed that he had a good ear and natural talent for music. I explained that I would help her with him. We would talk with him more frequently, show him that he was loved very much, and we would encourage him. We could do this if we stuck together. She agreed. Everything was going to be alright.

    Time passed and Christmas Eve was upon us and the ritual family gatherings were in order. I had my visits to make and Jess had hers. We put up a tree at the house and were excited to share it together as a family. Deciding when we would celebrate together was the big question. On the Eve, they always went to her mom's house for dinner and stayed the night to have Christmas morning breakfast and gift exchange. My schedule was a bit more open. Most of my family was dead, so no commitment there. Maybe I would see my brother or aunt and uncle for a couple of hours if they were well enough to get together. I was always invited to spend time with the Bitar family and could drop by whenever I wanted. There was no real set plan or pressure. They just didn't want me to be alone, especially on the holidays. This meant a lot and I always made it a point to see them. To our surprise, Jess's mother said, "Rather than the usual over-night stay, perhaps you should be with Sylvia to spend your first Christmas together." We were shocked and relieved that a huge weight had been lifted from us. She was slowly coming around! We were so happy and thankful! That morning was special. I enjoyed watching her son open gifts from us and from Santa. It was cool to see his eyes light up when he opened something he really wanted. In fact, he seemed to light up about everything he got! My heart was so warm. This was good stuff!

CHAPTER 9

REACHING FOR THE SUN

AFTER THE HOLIDAYS, MY future step-son expressed an interest in martial arts. My first thought was discipline. Yes! Something positive! "That's great! Let's sign you up!" I encouraged him by paying for the classes, buying any gear he needed and taking him there. At first, he was totally excited. He loved the uniform and the defensive moves he learned and wanted to go just about every day. I made a deal with him and said, "As long as your homework is done, I will take you as often as you like." I never saw homework get done so fast! Of course, when a kid tries something, the novelty tends to wear off quicker than adults would like. He had it in his head that this was going to be more of a social event for talking and making friends. When he realized this was not the case and there was demand from the Master to listen to instructions and pay attention …well, …so much for the intense interest. Getting him to go to class once a week became a battle. Needless to say, martial arts training came to an abrupt end.

In the meantime, coming to light was a new-found discovery that my girl drank a little too much, too often. I found myself getting her son off the bus while she made her usual pit stop at the bar after work. At first, it wasn't a big deal. This was her routine. She worked hard and earned the right to do what she wanted and came home a little buzzed. I didn't say anything right away in fear that I would be misunderstood and taken as a controlling asshole of a partner. But within a couple of months residing together, I watched her completely change course. Our relationship took on an ugly face that I recognized too well. Any intimacy in every form that I received from her had disappeared. I could feel her tension and wanted to talk about it. We NEEDED to talk about it, so we could figure out exactly what the issue was and remedy the situation. The only thing she could say to me was, "I want to go home."

"What do you mean? You ARE home. What's going on?" My mind was blown away! Jess stated that she did not feel comfortable here. She interpreted my discipline of her son, (which should have been her job) as, "This is my house and you'll do as I say!" She couldn't have been more wrong. Jess's failure to communicate, left me completely in the dark. Now, I found out that she was unhappy, uncomfortable, and not knowing what to do about it. I longed to understand and fix the problem and urged the importance of communication between us so that we could figure it out. Jess agreed and reassured me that she loved me and was just having some funky feelings. This worried me. It worried me quite a bit. Was she doing it again? How could she? I remembered our talks about her being absolutely SURE that she wanted a life with me. My head was spinning and I had to focus on having faith in her. The next month went from bad to worse. The first week was good. The rest left me no choice but to say, "It's either me or the booze. I will not live with an alcoholic ever again." I described the horrible things I dealt with, relating to alcohol in my family, and that this was a deal breaker for me. I wanted to understand her distance and sudden change of heart. I expressed my love and gently nudged her to question herself again about what she wanted in her life. She cried in my arms and said that things would change. I wanted to believe it. I didn't know if she had it in her. I just wanted my girl back.

From that point, Jess cut her drinking down quite a bit. She was trying to prove to me that I was important to her and those efforts were comforting. I knew how hard it was to beat an addiction. I gave away my supply of alcohol to friends and abstained from any cocktails in support of her. In the back of my mind, there was a voice warning me that if she was only getting sober for me and not for HERSELF, there was going to be a problem. After a short time, I discovered I was right. I struggled, trying to figure out how someone who said the most loving things to me, like how wonderful I was and how she couldn't live without me, could turn stone cold in a matter of seconds. She was doing it again. Now, I was sure of it. Son of a Bitch!

It was clear to me now that Jess did not love herself and was incredibly uncomfortable in her own skin. She was therefore unable to maintain a healthy relationship with someone else. I recalled the insecurities she had in High School and realized that they were still with her. The logic and the "fixer" in me tried to convince myself that if she'd work on herself we would be fine." I shared some of the books that were a great help to me in my journey and she was receptive.

My mind was dizzied, trying to understand her. The only thing I knew for certain was what I was feeling. I spent hours attempting to decipher what I was experiencing and asked myself questions like, "What is my definition of love? Am I doing something wrong?" I again reflected on my family and knew that my understanding of what defined a healthy relationship was limited. I had an idea of what a loving partnership SHOULD be, which included being kind and supportive. Holding hands, looking each other in the eye and speaking honestly seemed important. Feeling safe, spending quality time together, watching a sunset, making love, cuddling, being thoughtful, or just plain enjoying each other's company in general seemed like a no brainer. This was not what we were living and all my beliefs were in question. My only life line was to believe in the honesty of her words and even that was in doubt. I had put all of myself into this and could not handle the stress as my world turned upside down.

Worried for myself, I went to the doctor and they prescribed antidepressants in the hopes of relieving my helplessness and anxiety. Instead, I found myself in a downward spiral. I was missing work a lot and juggling medications to find the right one. I was angry with myself and didn't understand why I was having such a hard time with all of this. I was such a strong person that had dealt with so many different situations and issues. I usually had a knack for keeping a clear head in the midst of turmoil. Apparently, this situation was the exception. One morning, I found myself lying in bed on a work day, home alone, body shaking, unable to move, and I could barely breathe. Unbearable pain weighed down my chest and I believed I was having a heart attack. By chance, a co-worker I was friends with called to check up on me. When she heard my shaky voice and the description of what I was experiencing, she knew I was in serious trouble. She insisted I should 'sit tight' until she got out of work and would take me where I could get the right help. Thankful, I waited and when she arrived, she helped me into her car for a ride to the hospital.

Upon arrival, she led me to the emergency room and we waited for what seemed like hours. Finally, after being interviewed, I was admitted to the Psych Ward for further evaluation and they stated that it would be best for me to stay a minimum of one week. I was glad I had quit smoking a year ago because it was total lock-down and I couldn't leave the hospital wing to go outside. They gave me something to sleep and my friend made some calls for me. One of them was to Jess, giving her my status and a phone number to reach me. They got into an argument and my friend spoke her mind, "It's not all about YOU right now! It's about Sylvia!" Jess didn't take to that very well, felt insulted, and worried more about herself. I was grateful that my friend stuck up for me. She was aware of everything I was sacrificing to help Jess and her son. Later that evening, Jess and I spoke on the phone and she was completely unsupportive. All she talked about was how angry she was because my friends knew how bad off I was, but didn't consider what SHE was going through. I was totally exhausted and flabbergasted that her concern was only for herself and about what other people thought of her. I lost all focus and couldn't take it. I had consumed myself with taking care of her and her son so completely that I forgot to take care of myself. The worst part was the knowing that I had so many people that loved me, family and friends, co-workers, and yet I felt completely alone, consumed in utter depression. I was living in the deepest part of hell.

Over the next few days, I was fed a bunch of different pills and asked, "How do you feel today?" My response differed depending on what pills they gave me. One day, I didn't want to come out of my room, another made me irritable, the third turned me into a zombie, and yet another made my anxiety worse. No matter the pill, I didn't want to eat and just thought about how nice it would be to have a fucking cigarette. Finally, they found the right mix of medications that seemed to be helpful and I started coming around. My focus slowly returned and I started to pay attention to the other patients around me and realized that my problems were minimal in comparison. I met some very interesting characters, to say the least, and said to myself, "I know I'm not THAT crazy!" Now, I hoped they would let me go home soon.

Friends visited and brought me new pajamas, puzzle books and munchies. As they looked at my surroundings, I could see concern in their eyes. Jess came to see me and brought clothes, basic necessities, a book and a stuffed animal. I was grateful to see her, though she was on edge the whole time. Upon reflection, I think she felt like she put me there. And to be honest, the situation DID put me there. It wasn't a blame game, it's just the way it was. My head was so confused over our situation and the 'Why's' that I was literally at a complete loss. A few more days passed and when we spoke on the phone, she sobbed, "I'm sorry! Everything will be fine baby. We'll take care of one another, we'll be open and honest, always talking and being positive. We can do a little extra every day for each other to show our love. I will not let my other stresses interfere with us and will work very hard to remove it or learn to place it elsewhere. You're too important to me and I will make you happy again and forever." Her son cried in the background and I requested to speak with him, "I will be home soon buddy. Don't you worry." They both cried, "Please come home. We miss you! Please come home!" And I did, a few days later. I returned to work a month later and attended counseling sessions once a week. My relationship with Jess improved and it seemed we were back on track.

Finally, there seemed some normalcy around the house. Jess quit drinking completely and I was proud of her. I knew it was no easy task. She needed to build her self-esteem and what better way than to conquer old, self-defeating habits. I supported her through it, even when it got rough. Her mother and friends noticed the change, and all thanked me, "You are a positive influence!" They told Jess that I was good for her and now she realized it. I didn't want credit. Jess had to do all the work but, there was a little piece inside of me that knew I had helped and that was enough.

Just when things were blossoming, Jess lost her job. To top it off, she was diagnosed with an incurable nerve disorder. To witness a loved one suffering is the most helpless feeling on the planet. Jess still carried the burden of low self-esteem and I was unable to talk her out of it. When she became unemployed and sick, she hit an all-time low. It wasn't noticeable at first. She seemed to be holding up and I assured her that we would get through it together and not to worry about money for the moment. We would address her health issues first and take things one day at a time. Sticking together was my frame of mind and the promise she made when I got out of the hospital. I thought she was on board.

The next few months were difficult for me. In the midst of the issues that Jess and her son were facing, I was trying not to set myself aside. "Weren't my own needs just as important as theirs?" I tried to painstakingly hold up the fort in all areas because she could not. Total support, kind words, love and thoughtfulness were not enough. She put up an impenetrable wall and I was not allowed in. There could be no significant connection made with someone who saw themselves as undeserving, fearful, doubtful, guilty, angry and unlovable. These things blocked the path to receive anything positive that was offered. This led to a discussion. We agreed that we moved in together too soon and this made her feel trapped. We held each other and cried, hoping that by living separately we would heal the relationship. The next few weeks were spent packing and looking for an apartment for her.

Jess found a place a few blocks away and I gave her my couch and a bed for her son. I was happy for her, knowing this was what she needed. I had a hard time letting her go but the silence in the house was actually soothing. I looked forward to starting over and interacting with Jess and her son on a healthier level. We agreed to do dinner every couple of weeks and work on the relationship slowly. A couple of months passed with next to no communication from her and I found myself depressed, sitting around waiting for the phone to ring, wondering if anything she said held any value. I was duped and dumped. One afternoon, I was standing next to my drum set when I dropped to the floor, weeping so hard that I lost my breath. On my knees, I raised my hands to the ceiling and pleaded for God to help us. I couldn't understand why she was sent back into my life only to walk away again, "This wasn't how it was supposed to be!" I was lost, and chastised myself for disregarding that I was already a whole person, with or without her. Deep down, I knew that our reunion was not for the reason I wanted. It was all about finding closure for the past by taking care of unfinished business: no more than that. My stubbornness could not accept this and I grew increasingly angry with Jess, with God, and with my life.

Anger can be so destructive. The more I sat around dwelling on things, the more it poisoned me. I knew I had to change my thinking. So, over the next year, I turned that anger into motivation and decided it was time to travel again. I hopped on a plane and went to New Mexico for a weekend. I took another road trip across the country with my friend Sarah and we explored the beauty and splendor of Yellowstone National Park. We spent the Fourth of July at Mount Rushmore and my eyes welled up as I first gazed upon it. As we traveled further, I was awed by Crazy Horse Monument and felt the loneliness of the earth in the Badlands. I captured some inner peace on this trip and realized that traveling was something I wanted and needed to do for my soul for the rest of my life. I was called to the place of my birth in Wisconsin on the way home and Sarah was happy to oblige. I sat next to a lake and meditated as the sun set…yearning to understand the events of my entire life. "It all started here," I said to myself, feeling like my parents were sitting next to me. At that moment, I was reminded that I had to accept everything for what it was and just allow life to unfold without expectations, or try to force things to go the way I wanted. A final thought blew through me, "Let go and trust the universe with all its mystery no matter what the circumstances! You are loved and protected. All is well, either way!" The gentle fingers of a warm breeze brushed my hair, filling me with the comfort and reassurance of a hug. I gave thanks and headed home.

I was amazed by the human mind and how easy it was to lose a good feeling and remembered the importance of daily positive self-talk. As I resumed daily routines of work, house chores and band practice, there still remained a loneliness that I couldn't seem to shake. I pushed myself forward even though I didn't have the drive to, and chose to continue working with my counselor. Two years had passed since my visit to the hospital. I had weened myself off just about all medications and was told that counseling was no longer necessary, but something told me to continue my involvement. I was frightened by the thought of ever returning to the depths of hell that had consumed me. When I involved myself in counseling and group work, I saw that my life wasn't half bad compared to some of these people and the suffering they faced. During this process, I realized how good it made me feel to help others. Sometimes, people in the group would address me rather than the counselor for advice. I remembered the friends that called upon me in the past. I began to think about my purpose and imagined how I could change the direction in my life and career to be of service to others.

That year, I took in a very lost girl who had an abusive boyfriend. She had nowhere to go and I could relate to this, so I opened my home and offered safety until she got on her feet. I discovered an inner happiness, through giving, and my gratitude grew to new heights for my house and the ability to help. I was getting better at listening to the voice within. Some people thought I was crazy for opening my home to someone I barely knew, but I knew it was the right thing to do. Her stay lasted about six months before she moved on. Later, she thanked me for my kindness and I was even more thankful that I had been able to help.

I continued to learn so much about mindfulness in counseling. One of the exercises we did was so basic, it was almost stupid, yet proved to be an eye opener. I was asked to give attention to my body sitting in the chair. Was I comfortable? Was I slouching? Could I feel the weight of my body being held up by the chair? Did my neck or shoulders feel tense? If so, I tried to relax. Was I clenching my teeth? Now, a piece of candy was offered to me. As I held it in my hand to unwrap, what color was the wrapper? Before I eat it, what does it smell like? Is it hard or soft candy? What does it taste like? Am I chewing it too fast?

I was blown away by how many thousands of things I did during the day that were done on auto-pilot. I thought about driving my car, arriving somewhere and not remembering the journey. Was there a lot of traffic? Was I speeding? Did I cut anyone off? Where was my mind when I was driving? Sounds pretty dangerous right? This is so common in everyone so I tried to apply what I learned earlier to my car. Before even taking off, how do my hands feel on the wheel? What is its texture? How does the seat feel? On and on, throughout the entire drive, I tried to notice everything. Getting stuck in traffic no longer bothered me because there were so many things to look at to pass the time.

By giving these simple little things a try, the connection to my surroundings, including my Spirit, was enhanced. My head feels less cluttered and I seem to be able to live in the present moment more often. Jess reappeared around Christmas time trying to rekindle our relationship and I fell prey for a short time. The beautiful words, the apologies, the sex, the explanations of how she healed herself. It was all bullshit! The end result was always the same . . . no follow through. That whole situation boiled down to a matter of MY self-love and self-respect. I had come too far and wasn't going to allow myself to be dragged down again. I already felt like the biggest fool on the planet for even considering the idea. I was present when she had an important surgery and I took care of her son in her absence. I straightened up their apartment for her return and looked around at all the familiarities. I knew this was the last time my eyes would look upon these things. "I wish you peace Jess." And with those words, spoken to the walls, I locked the door behind me and went home. It was time to completely let go. I had to for my own self-preservation.

My counselor was now giving me the official "boot", confident that I had all the tools I needed. The doctor only had one recommendation for me, and it was huge. Relocate to somewhere in the southwest and retreat to year-round sunshine. This meant a new job, a new life. The idea was welcomed and I found myself on the internet feverously searching for a job in my field. The thought of packing up was both exciting and dreadful. Did I sell my house or rent it out in case things didn't work out and I'd have a place to come back to? Where do I go? Would I be happy there? I got a job offer in New Mexico where my friend lived but there was a huge cut in pay and no medical insurance. It seemed too risky to give up everything. I really had it made right where I was. I had a great job, great friends and family which offered a huge support system. I agreed with the doctor about the year-round sunshine to put an end to what he called 'seasonal depression', but I was questioning all those years of struggle to get where I was. Was I being ungrateful somehow by wanting something more or different? Just because I had a life altering heartbreak didn't mean I had to leave town. Conflict clouded my mind. It seemed the wisest choice, for now, to stay put and yet a little voice cried, "Chicken! You will be stuck in the mud forever if things don't change!" Feeling confused, I prayed for guidance once again.

During this time of indecision, I remembered when I lived with my mother in chaos and discovered chakra balancing on the television. Coincidently, a friend invited me to check out place that hosted healing circles. I was intrigued and accepted the invitation.

As we parked the car, I felt a sense of excitement to experience something new and cool. When we walked in, there were at least a dozen people sitting comfortably on couches and cushy chairs arranged in a large U-shape. They were talking, laughing, and sharing stories as my friend and I found a place to plant ourselves. At first, I felt a little weird and as I listened to some of the conversations, I thought I was surrounded by some really strange birds! Eyes wide and eyebrows raised. I looked at my friend to see if she was catching the same vibe. She looked at me and giggled. Leaning close to my ear, she said, "Some people go way overboard but give it a chance." I tried to relax and set aside my judgements.

As I sat quietly at attention, a man started talking about the energy of the universe. I perked up with interest and joined the conversation, sharing my wonder of it all as the host entered the room to begin the healing circle. We were given little pieces of paper and asked to write down something we wished to be rid of. For example, "I wish to be rid of anxiety, a broken heart, drama, chaos, etc. Our wishes/prayers were put together in a bowl, later be burned or something symbolic like that. I interpreted it as a personal release; a letting go of something that clouded my mind and blocked me from moving forward in life. We joined hands to close the circle as the host said a prayer of blessings. She took us through a guided meditation as we closed our eyes and imagined we were walking through the woods to the stream of water she described. We were given choices. Would I drink the water? Bathe in it? Cross over it and keep going? As the guided journey continued, I was surprised that I was able to focus. My mind created vivid and beautiful details of my surroundings as I walked through the forest. The group that I held hands with had disappeared and I was a free spirit roaming this place of mystery and awe. Occasionally, my mind tried to sabotage the journey by throwing in a fear that a bear was up ahead and waiting for me, or that I was being followed by something malevolent. *Should I open my eyes? No! Just breathe and know that I am in control.* It worked! *How cool is this!* Eventually, we all had to open our eyes and return to the room. Going around the circle one at a time, we were asked to express what we were grateful for. My response reflected the peace I felt in that moment.

My friend and I wanted to explore further and took classes to study Reiki. We absorbed ourselves in the practice of natural energy healing and deeper meditation. I met some down to earth people that were easy to talk to and shared similar goals to my own. My main priority was, and will always be, maintaining balance within, and helping others to find their own personal power to heal themselves. I was again learning to become more mindful and this group work opened my eyes to truly focusing and feeling someone else's pain other than my own. I studied and practiced every day, and though I didn't give much worth to titles and badges, I earned two certificates, enabling me to be considered a Reiki Practitioner.

At forty-something-years-old, I finally felt whole. The idea of dwelling on anything negative became unattractive and I experienced an empowering freedom. I distanced myself from overly dramatic people with hyperactive gossip and limited my time watching the news on TV as well. Life became much more enjoyable! I didn't judge people who chose to live in chaos, I only knew that when I invested time there, I walked away exhausted and felt like an energy vampire bit and drained the life out of me. I was completely sick of it!

I was refreshed and excited to continue decluttering my life and chose to be more kind to myself. If I forgot to keep my mind in check and took a few steps backwards into dark or self-defeating thoughts, I learned to laugh at myself or the situation by saying something like, "OMG! There I went again! How long was I gone?" Rather than beating myself up with convincing words that I'd never get it right or nothing changes, I gave thanks that I was able to notice it, regroup, and move on. I realized the absurdity of carrying around emotionally charged baggage and decided to sit with the pain of each event in my life, one at a time, from the far past and forward, to understand their true value. No one wishes to relive the pains of the past and it seems that the best thing to do for yourself is to bury it deep and far beyond the realm of conversation. Yet, I found the consequence of diving into the pain and darkness led to the unearthing of more wonderful qualities about myself that I had not given credit to . I was reminded to adopt yet a new appreciation of my spirit.

I compared myself to a rambunctious primate and laughed at how my mind could still carry on with constant brain chatter. This had been consuming way too much of my time without my being conscious of it. You would think that, with all of the mindfulness work I'd done so far, I should be cured of this huge annoyance. I've come to the conclusion that being human includes many primordial features and the "monkey mind" takes center stage!

I thought about the time Sarah and I went to Devil's Tower in Wyoming and hiked up as far as we could go. There were enormous boulders all along the base and I found myself completely in the moment as I concentrated on the task at hand. It was so empowering to experience 'The Now' ALL day long! I climbed carefully, paying attention to every forward motion and every rock ledge of which to reach and grab onto. I felt as if I was "one-with" the Tower and my surroundings. It was incredible! I noticed a Raven fly by and land on a tree branch to observe me. I noticed every nook, every crack. Hell, I noticed everything! I playfully followed a chipmunk through the twists and turns of my ascent under the beautiful blue sky. This was one of the most enlightening spiritual experiences I ever had. I paused to sit and contemplate this tranquil moment. My body resonated with awe and gratitude. Everything around me was in perfect harmony and I was a part of it all! How wonderful to be fully aware in the presence of gentleness and unconditional love! I knew it was imperative to dedicate my life to the practice of mindfulness and to walk the path of inner truth, even if I faltered.

CHAPTER 10

IN FULL BLOOM

BY MY MID-FORTIES, THERE was a huge difference in the flow of my life, due to the work I put into myself and by keeping the company of positive people. I noticed that I was now attracting more synchronicities and joyful experiences. The new people I met were interesting and full of life. By happy coincidence, I reconnected with a long-forgotten acquaintance. Violet and I bumped into each other at a supermarket and were WOWED with one another! It was so nice to see her and we chatted briefly, making it a point to get together. We exchanged phone numbers with wide-eyed excitement and contacted each other soon afterwards. We met frequently for dinner and rekindled our friendship.

There was something about me and Violet that was magnetic. When we didn't see each other, we were always texting and when we managed to get together, it was incredibly fun! We couldn't seem to get enough of each other's company! The time passed so quickly when we were together, and I remember both of us being amazed by that. Everything was shared without judgement and we talked extensively about deep issues with empathetic ears. It was so refreshing to be in such good company!

Violet was supportive as I took interest in furthering my education in areas of the Healing Arts. I added a Sound Healing certificate to my list of credentials and, because I was a musician, this modality seemed very fitting. I learned how to use a pendulum and various tuning forks as tools to shift and balance energy in and around the body. I wasn't studying the Healing Arts to open a business. . . I studied for MYSELF! My desire to explore all avenues, discovering techniques or practices that would assist in my life, was absolutely fascinating and far from boring.

Right around this time, I decided to take the doctor up on his recommendation of investigating a move to the south-west. I took leave from work and it just so happened that one of my co-workers needed a place to stay. He was a gentle, sweet, and trustworthy person, so I took him on as a new roommate He would watch the cats and the house while I was away on what I now call a "vision quest". I was amazed by the way things just fell in line to make this journey possible. It was like I was supposed to go.

On my last day of work, the adrenaline surged as I thought about driving across the country by myself. It was exciting and I felt completely out of my mind for doing it. My thoughts were, "Did my forty-three-year-old mind just hit middle age crisis? Am I afraid of being stuck and looking to run away, only to find the same old shit? Was the doctor right about my feeling better in year-round sunshine? Maybe, I just need a break to nurture myself and explore some possibilities. Yes!" This was the thought I chose to run with. When I punched the time clock and headed to my car, a dove was sitting on my sunroof. I paused and sat on the curb, watched it, and sensed a vibe that this was going to be a peaceful and eye-opening journey.

In astonishment of the timing and its symbolism, I said, "Thank you," to the dove as a couple of co-workers in the parking lot noticed and shared my amazement, "Look Sylvia! It's a good omen! Wow! That's so cool!"

It was intoxicating to be driving alone with the car packed, my cooler full of drinks and snacks next to me on the front seat, and my I-Pod cranking through the car stereo on shuffle. It was loaded with ALL types of music, but I noticed that relevant and positive songs streamed one after the other, coinciding with the present moment and the wonderous thoughts in my head! My hair stood up on my arms as the Universe was playing DJ for me! Song after song, I couldn't help but smile! I thought about how blessed and thankful I was right down to my core! I thought about Violet and how awesome it would be if she was with me.

Since I was driving through, I decided to make a pit-stop in Colorado to visit my grammar school pal Addy, and then on to see my other long-time friend Jane. It just so happened that they both moved to the same city but, for years, were unaware of each other's whereabouts. These girls were a sight for sore eyes and what a great beginning for a soul-searching trip! One day, the three of us got together and reminisced, laughing the whole time about all the shenanigans we, or should I say I, caused. Both of them took the time to turn me on to a few interesting and beautiful areas during my short stay. My friends were doing well here, and I wondered if Colorado would be a potential place to plant my feet.

Before heading off to Arizona, I stayed the night at Jane's house. She had not been feeling well and told me that doctors were in the process of investigating something that appeared on an x-ray of her belly. She expressed her discomfort in detail and I wished that I could do something to help. The only thing I had to offer was Reiki. Jane knew what that was and eagerly accepted my offer for a healing session. I put on some soothing music as she laid down on her back and got comfortable. I approached and quietly said a prayer, gave thanks, and asked for assistance to help my friend. I could feel a vibrating warmth between my hands and moved them, above her body, to scan her energy centers/chakras for a sensation of imbalance. As I listened from within for guidance, there was a heaviness in my hands over her forehead, heart, and abdomen. I focused on each of these areas individually, envisioning colored light pouring into these centers, charging them up like a battery. Then, the thought of her grandparents came to mind, so without questioning it, I asked her about them. Tears rolled down her cheek and she was surprised by this. Apparently, there still remained some forgotten negative emotions that weighed her down. This realization opened the door to reflection and an acknowledgement of what she no longer needed to carry around with her. As I listened to her story, I could feel stagnant energy lifting from her body, leaving her in a state of comfort and peace. I closed our healing session with another prayer of thanks.

Later that evening, terrible pain in my belly consumed me and I vomited throughout the night. Jane and I later joked that it was some sort of exorcism! When she went back to the doctor for another x-ray and further testing, there was nothing there and her symptoms were gone. She and I were both amazed! I was happy knowing that, through the constant practice of listening from within, I was able to open my mind to the power of love and be a conduit of help and service from that which is beyond. I was humbled and so thankful! What a great start on my journey to Arizona!

I splurged to spoil myself and rented a house for an entire month called "Castle Sedona." It wasn't really a castle but the size of it might as well have been. The place sat directly on a mountainous red rock and it was spacious and beautiful with tons of character. I smiled as I pulled into the driveway, gazing at the awesomeness of the landscape. I laughed out loud when I saw the meditating Buddha next to the front entrance holding the house key for me. Eager to explore, I entered my temporary home and couldn't believe the great vibe here. Every area of the house was full of inspiration! The first floor was completely open and while I cooked in the kitchen, I could see the huge fireplace. Windows facing the backyard stretched from floor to ceiling, bringing the brilliance of the red rocks and cacti into full view. I chose the second-floor bedroom as my resting place because there were French doors that opened to a balcony overlooking the backyard and towering landscape. This was the perfect view to set my eyes on first thing in the morning! As I unpacked, I saw two gorgeous hawks gliding free and easy above the red peeks against the solid deep blue sky. I knew that I would be spending most of my time out in the yard.

It was truly magical here and there was a peace washing over me that I'd never felt before. My senses were keen, my mind was present, and my heart was completely alive as the coyotes howled and the owls whooed in the moon light. Butterflies and hummingbirds joined me for morning coffee every day and fluttered in front of my face, as if to say, "Good morning!". Ravens watched and cawed wherever I went. Dragonflies and roadrunners zipped around the yard, bringing a smile to my face. One particular morning, a bobcat stopped fifteen feet away to listen and watch me play a Native American flute! In that moment, I wasn't sure if I was on her breakfast menu. We looked each other in the eye and, in my mind, I thanked her for her enchanting presence. I continued to play and she stayed for a short while before moving on. I was pleased with myself that I decided to spend more money than I wanted to rent this place! It was an absolute treat and well deserved. This was something I would never regret!

I brought a journal and hoped to record everything I experienced while in full relaxation mode. I bought a Native American book that explained the spiritual meanings of the animals that crossed my path. I was astonished that ALL were in sync with my life at that time, full of good omens and positive energy. I was excited to share my findings with Sarah. She was on this end of the country and made her way to visit me. We shared some great candlelight dinners with wine at the Castle and played a lot of music out in the yard with the sun shining and drink glasses full. Every night Sarah was there, we had a bon-fire under the stars. We laughed as we quickly retreated to the house if we heard howling or strange sounds coming from the blackness beyond the reach of the fire. I was a little kid again!

Sarah and I spent time hiking through the gorgeous vortex areas in Sedona and my favorite was Cathedral Rock. There are spires in the center of the butte that look like two people standing with their backs to one another. A stranger told me a story that a couple went hiking and had a terrible argument. As they stood with their backs turned in stubbornness to speak to one another, the sun set, and they turned to stone. Moral of the story; never go to bed angry with your partner. Cool! There was so much to learn here. The area around Cathedral Rock was loaded with beautiful trails and I found a favorite spot under a giant Sycamore tree, right next to a body of mirror-like fresh water. I gazed into the creek amongst the splendor and quietly observed the red rock skyline reflection as the ravens watched me. It is said that when you are in a vortex, everything is amplified. If you're feeling good, you will feel even better. If you feel depressed or aggravated, this will also be amplified. I was feeling thankful. My prayers were deep, honest and filled with emotion, asking to draw in more positivity and healing for myself. With that, I was inclined to place my hands in the cold water, creating a ripple. I cupped my palms together, scooped up a handful, and watched as it fell through my fingers. Another scoop, and I washed my face. And yet another, to hold it and then slowly pour it back to where it came. I knew my prayers were heard when the water stilled, and I could again see my reflection.

Later that week, I discovered another area that I explored alone called Boynton Canyon. I took a backpack and my journal on several occasions to meditate in this powerful vortex. I climbed up to a comfy spot in the shade, under a twisted tree located between two spires, in search of more spiritual awakening. A local man sat in the distance, atop a red sandstone formation called Warrior Rock, and beautifully played a wooden flute. The stillness was tingling! I moved into the sun and laid my body onto the solid earth between the two spires and closed my eyes. The warm ground on my back soothed me even further as I felt a gentle wind wash the waves of the flute song over my body, penetrating every muscle. I dozed off and when I awoke, the flute player approached and gave me a heart-shaped red rock. "You will find these everywhere, if you look," he said, before disappearing down the trail. As I gathered my things and hiked out of the box canyon, I saw them everywhere! I looked to the sky and said, "Thank you!" My desire to live here grew to new heights and I decided to do more research on cost of living, housing, and submit resumes for employment.

As I waited for response to my inquiries, I attended some healing circles to address issues of the heart. Though I had come a long way, I still felt as if I had been impaled and had a hole right through my chest. Something was wrong or missing but I just couldn't pinpoint it. When I participated in a group Reiki session, the healers even felt it without my saying anything.

"Wow! What's going on in your heart dear?"

The Reiki master called to her fellow practitioners. "Come here and tell me what you feel."

Hands were placed over my heart chakra and after a moment, tears ran down their cheeks. "Whatever it is honey, you have to let it go!"

I still couldn't figure it all out. *It can't just be my recent break-up.* I deduced that it must have been years and years of accumulated heartache stemming back to childhood. But *I thought I dealt with all that! Hmm. Now*

I'm at a complete loss. Yet, the more I spent time exploring this mystical land of Sedona and her inhabitants, the more a comfort washed over me and that hole in my heart began to fill itself up again.

As I basked in the good vibes during moments of deep contemplation, I wasn't convinced that I would find a long lasting and loving partner, but I would adopt a positive attitude to keep the door open. I thought about Violet and how enamored we were with one another, but she wasn't gay and she wasn't single. These two things were obviously major roadblocks. The talks and texting with her throughout my time spent in Arizona made me wonder. But instead of entertaining a daydream, I let it go and focused completely on myself. This was the best medicine! I reflected on how I dropped my fears and followed through with this voyage, proving to myself that I was completely in charge of my own life and mind. It didn't matter where I was in the world and as my stay in Sedona was coming to a close, I wasn't overly disappointed when the job search didn't bear fruit. Something told me that everything would be OK.

One of my last nights at Castle Sedona was spent alone under the stars enjoying a bon-fire. I put my I-Pod on shuffle again and turned it up as I sipped on a cocktail, watching the sun set. I gazed longingly at the red rocks and gave thanks for ALL of it as the colors diminished to black and the twilight sky turned to moon and stars. One of my mother's favorite songs came on and I fell into a dead stare, mesmerized by the dancing and flickering of the fire in front of me. A soft warm breeze stirred and gently stroked my hair. She was here with me in my solitude and a wave of peace washed over me as another song from the far past rang through. I noticed the relevance of the lyrics and sang out loud as if we were reminiscing and singing along together. I talked to her and thanked her for this special moment. I told her that I forgave her for any misguided decisions in the past and said that I would not be who I am today without experiencing all of it. I apologized for ever making her feel unloved in our last few years together. I knew she understood and for the next hour, I smiled, laughed, and enjoyed the songs that kept coming, wave after wave of pertinence. Her visit touched every fiber in my being and I could feel her slowly pulling away, leaving me with a final message saying. "Wherever I go, I take you with me." Words cannot express my gratitude or the "cool factor" that night brought!

The next morning, I sat with a cup of coffee, watching the red rocks slowly return to their brilliance. A tear rolled down my cheek as I knew

I needed to pack up and leave. (A dove is cooing as I write this …how awesome!) I had a good job back home, stability, and a great network of supportive friends and extended family. There was a knowing in me that said, "I will be back, Sedona!". Now, was just not the right time and by accepting this and trusting the Universe, I would allow my life to start unfolding without trying to force my will. This frame of mind felt like a total truth and I enjoyed going along for the ride.

As I traveled home enjoying the scenery, I enjoyed complete rejuvenation and was excited and determined to permanently apply this energy to my life back home. As I journeyed down the highway, I was totally focused on gratitude and astonished that my mind had no desire to entertain the idea that this trip was a failure, just because I wasn't making a move. Every time I thought about Violet, I noticed that the speedometer reading jumped passed 100mph. I laughed at myself in my impatience to get home, "Well, isn't THIS something! I wonder what THAT'S all about?"

When I pulled in my driveway, I looked at the surrounding red brick buildings and smiled, "These are my red-rock mountains!" From that point, everything seemed to change for the better and I was happy to see and feel the results of my changed attitude. My monotonous job became more bearable and I resumed my music endeavors with the band. I stayed involved with meditation and energy work as I found a satisfaction in decluttering forgotten areas of my house. I went through box after box in the attic and thinned out the closets. I organized and repacked anything of significant sentimental value and tossed the rest. Old photos, clothes, furniture, memorabilia, whatever items that were not useful or couldn't put a smile on my face, went for donation. As I took on this task, I was decluttering not only my house, but my mind and spirit as well. Getting rid of unnecessary "stuff" by cleaning out my closets made room for new clothes, and it also made room in my head to allow for new experiences.

My roommate was inspired by the stories of my travels and asked me for a Sound Healing session. I was happy to oblige and asked him to give serious thought to what it was he truly needed. As he laid comfortably on the massage table and I began the work, I asked him to keep an open mind to all possibilities and to just go with it. I explained that the session would be most successful by paying attention to emotions and sensations in the body rather than listening to the mind question and doubt the experience.

This would help in finding what he was looking for. As I held the colored tuning forks upside down over his body, I clanked them together and they rang out and swirled over his main chakra energy centers. They are located in the middle of the body in a line starting from the base of the spine and extending through the top of the head. (There are tons of books on this that are an interesting read)!

My roommate declared that he was feeling waves of electric energy in different areas of his body. His hands and feet tingled as an overall sensation of calm overtook him. Then, he recalled a personal pain from the past and we placed our focus there to embrace its discomfort. "It's time to clear this negative energy out and give yourself space. Let's fill this empty space you have created with loving and positive energy that will serve to refresh you!" About an hour later, as our session came to a close, his body was sunk into a comfortable state of relaxation. He seemed drunk and slightly dizzied as he sat up and looked around the room. I urged him to rise slowly and flush his system by drinking a lot of water. Before leaving the table, his eyes grew wide and he couldn't stop talking about this profound experience. By allowing himself to "let go" and "let in", he experienced the power of self-healing (with just a little guidance from my end). The next day, he exclaimed, "I have never slept better!" In the following days and weeks, he was at ease and his joyfulness became contagious.

My buddy later shared with me, after moving out and changing jobs, that he was a changed man. After what he called, the "Blingy Blingy" experience with the tuning forks, he became more receptive to other people's feelings and, by creating space in his heart, he discovered the power of moving on and moving forward. With that, he chose to live in full awareness and found a loving partner to share his life with. A soothing warmth spread in my chest and my inner voice gave thanks for being a part of his healing process. I folded my hands on my lap, in consideration of my own current affairs.

Violet was in a committed relationship, but the draw between us was too overpowering and for two years, we became romantically involved. My heart sang again, which surprised me. I had come to terms with being alone and did not expect this. But, there was a truth about the love we shared that was, without question, strong and genuine. Everyone we kept company with saw it. We fit together like a glove and never once had a bad feeling or thought about one another. All we cared to do was spend our time and do everything together. It was invigorating! She was beautiful inside and out and I was thankful that we made each other feel alive again.

When Violet expressed that I made her life complete, I was so ecstatic and yet, I realized that my life could NOT be if she didn't make the decision to leave the routine life of her committed relationship and live from the heart with me. I adored her so much that I denied my own morals and values so that she could have everything she wanted and needed, in the hopes that, eventually, she would choose me.

As time passed, I realized that Violet was unable to give up her comfort zone and, as hard as it was, I walked away in order to be authentic to myself. The false hope that kept me in the clouds turned into wisdom. Intimate relationships are terrific but need to be healthy for BOTH parties. My stubbornness in wanting to make things to work out the way I thought they SHOULD, stemmed from WAY back and had always trumped common sense. I now had a full understanding of all my past relationship blunders.

When I thought of Violet, it stung. There was still a longing for her love and companionship. We remained friends, but it was hard for me. She was the "what if" woman and occasionally, I had to remind myself that I was good enough and we were perfect. It just wasn't meant to be. At least I knew I was strong enough to not compromise my spirit again, even if this meant being alone. I no longer look at this as fault. I have finally found happiness within myself! I am no longer saddened by the kind intentioned words of others when they say, "You deserve a good partner! I really hope you find her." I am open to this, and perhaps I will find her, but I don't NEED to. It is so empowering to feel that difference!

I kept my promise to nurture my spirit and nothing works better for me than being out in nature. I took a one-week vacation to California and met Sarah for a costal exploration. She rented a new Camaro Convertible for me, knowing that I was into muscle cars, and we drove from Malibu, all the way up Highway Pacific 1 to the Oregon border and back. The gorgeous scenery was unparalleled and I found it cleansing to breathe in the salty ocean air as we stopped frequently to admire areas like Santa Barbara, Big Sur, San Francisco, Mendocino, and Trinidad.

When we traveled through Humboldt and up through "The Avenue of the Trees", we stopped to walk amongst the giant Redwoods. I highly recommend this! We visited a few of the touristy areas, of course, and gazed upon some of the largest and oldest trees. These colossal beauties brought tears to my eyes as I felt the presence of Mother Nature herself! We were called further up the road to a place a little more secluded and with each step I took, something gave me the feeling that I needed time alone. Sarah understood this and went on her own exploration as I slowly strolled through this ancient forest. The vibe here was powerful!

As I ventured forward in bewilderment, I was so small amongst these giants! They were here long before me and held a certain quiet wisdom that was humbling and I sensed I was in the company of royalty. I hugged them, felt their essence, and saw that they were perfect in every way. I asked if they could share some knowledge with me and as I walked further, I happened upon an area that long ago had burned. A sadness flowed through me for the loss and as I continued, some trees were toppled over with their roots exposed, lying dead. I thought about my family. With further examination, I couldn't believe the beauty of these exposed roots! (The dove is cooing again as I write this! Cool!) The intricate weaves, hollows, and exposure of these ginormous anchors now took on the appearance of mystical flowers.

I thought about my own roots and what was once buried. I said to myself, "These too, are beautiful flowers of my life." I wandered further and stumbled upon a Redwood standing tall with its core completely burned out. I approached and stepped inside this cavern of sorts and looked up into the center of the tree. Charred and empty it was, stretching upwards through its heart, almost reaching the sky. A sad and yet amazing sight that it still stood. I stepped out and noticed that there was new growth on its trunk, as if trying to heal and strengthen itself, particularly around its gaping wounds. I was overwhelmed with waves of gratitude and inspiration. This was me! At one time, my insides felt completely destroyed, burned out, and yet I also stood. When I stepped into the hollow of that tree, it was like stepping into myself. I was unequivocally convinced of the absolute importance of "going within" to see and feel the damage done, face the facts with compassion, and accept everything without judgement to find its value, allowing wounds to heal over time.

I could again see everything around me with perfect clarity and understanding that I was not separate from the divine. This was yet

ANOTHER moment of truly finding my 'self' and being thankful for the REMINDER to let go and allow without expectation! I thanked the Ancient Redwood Forest for allowing me to see and feel the whole picture. There is nothing more powerful, amazing and beautiful!

It is so easy to get distracted and forget about our own personal peace and truth. I know that occupying this human body, equipped with an ego and fuel injected emotions, blinds us. Walking around in a trance leads to being lost in a dark world with the belief that this is all there is. I no longer find this acceptable for myself. I hope that others can relate and find the motivation to discover the love hidden deep within …to rise above all obstacles and live an empowered life. I can say for certain that by projecting positivity, compassion, and loving energy, the same returns to you in one form or another. Closure and unanswered questions start to find YOU. My recent visit to Sedona proved it.

It was great to be back in this place again for my forty-eighth birthday. As usual, it felt like home and I gave thanks for yet another visit. One morning, I sat quietly outside with my coffee amidst the beauty of the red mountains. I contemplated my sensation of being connected to all that I saw and that there is access to all possibilities. During this present and peaceful moment, something completely out of the blue happened and it lifted me to a place of the greatest awe and gratitude. As I sipped my coffee and listened to meditation music in a state of bliss, my phone chirped. A woman from the far past, with whom I wished to speak with all my life, messaged me on Facebook. It was my step-mother. I couldn't believe the timing! I was in the process of writing this book and there were holes in the story. More importantly, there were unfulfilled curiosities that plagued me. I never thought I would have the conversation I needed with her. I am SURE that because my mind was completely open to all possibilities in that moment, it allowed this time of healing to come through. We chatted briefly and exchanged phone numbers, agreeing to set a date for a get-together. She wanted to give me a couple of my father's things and look through her old photos together. I was so excited, and a flood of memories poured in. I wondered if she would see my father in me. I couldn't get home fast enough!

It turned out that my step-mother only lived about an hour away from me. I packed up the photos I had and drove down the highway with the radio cranked. I was joyful and nervous all at once as the Universe decided to

DJ again and played songs that reminded me of my father. Cruising further up the road, motorcycles roared, and goosebumps lifted my skin, "Hey Dad! Did you set this up?" The city turned to country and the hills waved their mighty Pine trees to greet me. I arrived and pulled onto a long dirt driveway, following it up to an open area filled with wild flowers. I parked and walked towards a woman sitting on the patio under a tree. We looked at one another in amazement, smiled, and embraced each other. I met her husband, who was very sweet, and then invited to sit and have a drink.

The next few hours were well spent looking through pictures I'd never seen, sharing family news, and listening to lots of stories about my dad when he was in college. She still had his Woodstock ticket stub. It was really cool to see that! I met my step-brother that I didn't know existed, who shared fond memories of my father as well. Step-mom and I drank a bottle of wine and that's when she told me, "I wondered if you were coming here because you were angry and thought that I stole your Dad away from your Mom. It wasn't like that." I said that I never considered it, but I did have questions. One by one, I inquired, leading up to the day of Dad's death. I didn't find out a whole lot more than I already knew, but I did get confirmation and clarification on many other stories that I had heard over time. Finally!

We sat down for dinner and as we talked and laughed together, I saw how she looked at me, examining my face as I smiled. She paid close attention to my animated gestures and humor. She recognized a piece of him in me and that made us BOTH happy. It must have been epic for her. It definitely was for me! She gave me some pottery that my dad made and gave me his biker belt. Before I left, she told her husband that if anything were ever to happen to her, she wanted me to have the pictures and the rest of Dad's things. We agreed to stay in touch and I left, forever thankful.

After this encounter, light was given to the darkness in my mind. Nothing feels better than closure. It was like the Universe said, "OK. She's trying. She is learning. She has done well. Let's take from her that final piece of baggage so that she is free." Well, I say Amen to that!

In reflection: I am thankful to my father for his influence in the four short years I knew him for being the cornerstone of my interest in the road to enlightenment and transcendence. Today, I still don't have it all figured out, though my curiosity wants to know everything when it comes to the nature of our minds and what we believe. Knowing that "one" way is not the ONLY way, I have enjoyed looking at everything from Energy Healing to Jesus, Buddha, and Allah. My thirst for knowledge led me to take a glance at Animal Totems and Native American beliefs. Wicca, Angels, Guides, Aliens, Karma, and past lives were just a few more included in the long list of exciting explorations in my quest for knowledge and understanding. I took the things that worked for me and left the rest behind so that I could continue to grow.

Being mindful is what really spoke to me and this is why I have explored all different types of meditation. There are practices to help me focus on the good qualities that I (and we all) already possess, so I can amplify my attention and grow in kindness and compassion. Other forms of meditation that have been even more helpful to me focus on areas of self-improvement: toning down my self-criticism, building my self-worth, no longer believing in the limitations that I THINK I have, and learning to have a healthy relationship with my mind and emotions. Books are a great resource but if you're not a reader, 'You Tube' has tons of stuff! Guided meditations, meditation music for balance, and recorded conversations about things like manifestation and the law of attraction.

I know I will always have endless questions, but most importantly, I have finally found a certain calm in collaborating with the "not knowing" of things. Rather than fighting with myself, letting go and allowing has given me a better ability to cope. I can now place my trust in the synchronicities of life, knowing for certain that coincidences should not be ignored or written off as just a freak thing. Answers are all around us if we can be still and pay attention long enough to hear them.

As my journey continues through mid-life and events unfold hour by hour, day after day, it's no longer cumbersome. I can now say that I look forward to each fascinating day. Old memories rarely have a negative charge to them anymore and it feels so good to not be stuck in the mud! I know that I will encounter hang-ups, because shit just happens. I might struggle with emotional chaos when I forget myself and don't notice my personal, subtle reminders that keep me on track. Yet, how refreshing to know that I can bounce back quickly with mindfulness, embracing the power to overcome, and create my own better life experience! We ALL have this within our grasp. The best place to start is to ask yourself what you wish to be free of. It's time to take out the garbage!

CHAPTER 11

MOVING MOUNTAINS

I SAT, UNWINDING FROM the day with a cup of coffee and a cigarette, hoping for a second wind to blow my way to sweep me off this rocking chair to do something rewarding. The monotony of the work day had sent me into a paralyzing gaze with eyes glued to a fly on the window pane, buzzing and bumping into the glass in hopeless attempts of reaching the open air to be free.

"What a dummy," I thought to myself. "The window to your left is wide open! Can't you see with all those eyes on your head? Can't you feel the breeze swirling and streaming through the room to lead you out?"

I stared at this silly fly for quite some time and wondered why it wouldn't let go of the brightness beyond the glass and follow the wind instead. It would surely lose steam and dry up, only to fall dead on the window sill and meet my vacuum cleaner hose. And then I laughed, "Right now, I'm no smarter than you!"

The sounds of life beyond my window rang with a siren in a hurry to get somewhere. As it faded off in the distance, a train whistled so loud that it set off a car alarm in its wake. *I wonder where it's going? What's in tow? Is the train operator just as bored with his job as me?* The clanging of the steel wheels against the long and winding rails slowly echoed and then disappeared, leaving a stillness for a moment, allowing the hollow coos of a dove to be acknowledged.

My thoughts began to linger on writing a new book called "Mindfulness Made Easy". Catchy! A wonderful thought that ALL people can become mindful. Then, I thought about how many years it took for me to understand; to see and feel the value of this love, peace, kindness, compassion, and to hold open arms to all possibilities. I thought about some people I know who don't seem to have much of a drive to do "personal work" on a consistent basis and said to myself, "How in the world can mindfulness be made EASY? It doesn't seem easy at all!" With the mind in constant conflict with (and creating) highly charged emotions that lead a person astray, it feels daunting to take on your own mind and challenge its opinions, wants, demands, scenarios and fears. Maybe the real question is, "How can I influence people to WANT to change?"

The only thing I could come up with was living my own life in awareness in the hopes that I set a good example. Good enough for folks having a real hard time to be inspired enough to work with themselves long enough to see a difference. Unfortunately for my little brother, there wasn't enough time for him to see his true potential.

Throughout the years, my brother and I grew apart. He was living with his father (whom I obviously didn't get along with) and too much time had passed. We missed out on so many things together, only occasionally chatting on the phone or brief holiday visits with our uncle. His father always urged him not to tell me, for whatever reason, about anything that was going on his life. As a result, my brother rarely communicated his feelings with me and I totally blamed this on his father for creating a rift. I loved him so much, worried all the time, and wished that I could reach him. Any connection, words of wisdom, and encouragement I had to offer as a big sister was tainted.

A couple of summers ago when I took him shopping, I expressed those things to him in the car while enroute.

"It really sucks that a wedge was driven between us after mom died. I love you so much and have always wanted the best for you! I know the age difference played a partial role. I moved out of mom's when you were only 7 years old. So many times, I wished that things were different and we would be super tight. All these years, my loving advice was taken as "preaching" and I'm sorry for the misunderstanding. I have always seen the good man that you are in your core. I don't know. I don't know if I'm explaining things right or whatever. It just fucking sucks!"

This time, he heard me. "No, you said it good. You have always been there when I REALLY need it!"

His words gave me comfort. We talked about when I helped him move into a rental house to get him and his girlfriend all set up. It was nice to help him sort out and organize his things as we talked, laughed, and worked on small projects together to prepare for his baby's arrival. I missed doing those things together with my little brother and was grateful for this reconnection. Now, I was becoming an aunt and my brother was including me in his life. I was over the moon!

He always wanted to have a child and now the time was near. I got a kick out of how much he was "nesting"; constantly cleaning, putting together the baby's room, buying everything that would be needed for the next 3 years! He even bought doubles of things like car seats and playpens to have at my house for when I babysat. I was happy for his assumption that I would help with the baby.

While awaiting the arrival of his child, he seemed different. One minute he was ultra-focused and then the next, completely distracted. He started calling old friends to apologize for anything he may have done to offend. He called me constantly, which I had no problem with, though this was unusual. I figured he was excited, scared and overwhelmed all at the same time. I would be supportive and do anything I could to help.

The day my brother's son was born, he sent my pictures throughout the process in his hospital garb. He looked so proud to be a daddy, holding his newborn son, smiling and starring into his eyes as the baby smiled back at him. I couldn't wait to meet the little nugget! I hopped in the car and drove to the hospital to find mommy, daddy and baby completely passed out. Immediately, I approached the baby bed, leaned close and gently said, "Well hello! Welcome to the world beautiful!" He responded with a sweet little smile and opened his eyes. I spent every day for the next week visiting him.

I knew my brother was going to be a loving father as I watched in awe at how careful he was while changing diapers and buttoning up those tiny snaps on the baby's pajamas with his large hands.

"Who would've thought that we'd be doing THIS together," I said as we exchanged smiles.

Any time the baby stirred, my brother picked him up and the "nugget" was instantly calm and content. There was no doubt that the baby loved his voice. Even before entering the world, he always responded with a shift or kick when he heard his daddy talking to him in the womb. I felt so blessed sitting on the couch with my brother, playing with my nephew, sharing precious time and giggling together at the cute expressions on that sweet little boy's face.

I remembered when I bottle fed my baby brother and how enamored I was with him. As my nephew suckled on my chin, my brother exclaimed, "He doesn't do that for anybody!" I was filled with a joy in my heart that I had not experienced for many years. I suddenly felt a sense of rebirth and purpose. An unexplainable, overwhelming feeling took me over. Something deep inside of me vowed to love him, protect and watch over him for all of my life. My mind traveled back to the unbreakable bond I had with my grandmother. I sensed that my nephew and I would share the same.

A month later, due to brain trauma, my brother was gone. The scene was a repeat of my mother dying in the hospital with all of us there to bear witness. When I first saw him, held his hand and spoke with the doctor, I collapsed, threw up, and wound up in a hospital bed in the room next to him until I could stand without blacking out. They tried to save my little brother, but when he was declared brain dead, a decision had to be made. His girlfriend, my step-father and I held him as he departed to meet his maker. The disbelief, pain, anger, and inconsolable grief hit us all like a train. Friends of mine had to come and pick us up from the hospital.

I was now walking through a thick fog while working with my stepdad to make final arrangements. His drinking went way overboard for months as he cried himself to sleep every night. I couldn't blame him. This was his son. I had a few drinks myself in attempts to numb the pain and, for the first time ever, felt compassion for Mario. I know he had a lot of regrets and at first, out of anger, I hoped that he would be haunted by them as memories flooded my mind with the poison of the past. But now, we were sharing a similar pain. Now, we felt heartbroken, not only for the loss of my brother, but for the baby too.

I wasn't surprised when I fell into a deep depression. Getting out of bed to go to work on a regular basis became impossible. Migraine headaches were a constant and most days, I could not get out of bed. Though I was thankful for my job, the monotony and energy drain from having to interact with some real shitty personalities was completely unfulfilling. I found myself on a park bench with my journal rather than working, doing everything I could to relax and go easy on myself.

The breeze certainly felt good under the shade of a beautiful tree and the sun peeked through in an attempt to brighten the dismal sky.

"I'm glad, almost proud of myself for coming here today," I said aloud as my eyes welled up, against my will, every few moments. "The only thing I can do is just go with it for now."

A man played with his children on the playground and all were happy, full of life, vitality, love, and joy. I recognized these things and missed it. Even in the midst of the excitement of finishing and publishing a book, it was difficult to hold on to any joy or sense of accomplishment that was supposed to accompany it. I hoped that these sad times would not be long lasting. My friends all agreed that I had been through a lot. I recalled when a good friend, filled with loving compassion, said to me, "Dam! How much can a person take?" She hit the nail on the head. That's exactly what I was thinking.

In the park that day, I furiously wrote in my journal and this is what flowed through my pen.

To all that share the burden of depression. For those that feel they are no longer the life of the party but rather just a negative vibe that brings people down in your presence. For those who are disgusted with themselves for not being able to snap out of it. . . that have random, seemingly uncontrollable thoughts of what it would be like if you weren't here. . . all in search of relief because you're so fed up because pills, positive affirmations, and folks that love you cannot help you escape your persona hell. Wow! Shall I go on?

Giving advice on what will help you seems futile, coming from another depressed person, but I do find that going out into nature helps. Even if there is no park to go to, get outside to seek something larger than yourself. To breathe in the fresh air, to listen to the sounds of the breeze in the trees, the call of the birds, make pictures in the clouds, share your lunch with a squirrel, watch in wonder as the ants are busy searching for something, and absorb yourself in these things, even for brief moments, to get out of your head.

Write down your observations. You are, after all, an expert in this area and have plenty to say. We tend not to want to share our pain but this is why we are the best advice givers, the best comedians, the fixers, the most creative. Admire the masterpiece you truly are!

The blinding haze in my mind started to lift. I felt relief to be reconnected again. Within a month, something occurred to me that proved to be uplifting. There was definitely a fine line between coming to terms with something by going with the flow and swaying to the dark side of "I don't care anymore." In my bouts of depression, I've thought about my family and looked forward to meet them soon. I see their graves in my mind and envision the stillness of the landscape with all those stone-cold markers establishing permanent residence for these once physical entities that so shaped my life and fulfilled purposes of their own. I see my own name amongst them in the vast stone orchard, carved in granite, as a reminder to anyone who cares, that I once lived; that I shared a life with the names around mine, now forever silenced as the birds fly high above through the rays of the sun and await the rising of the full moon in the starlit sky. The day will certainly arrive without question and this vision will become my reality. So, what's the rush?

I tended to my thoughts and concluded that I have been blessed with time. Time to live a full life and honor my family/ancestors by experiencing this world and all it has to offer; sights, smells, touch, sounds that are all connected to a physical body that my family can no longer experience themselves. I am their direct connection to the earth, feeling the embrace of a hug, sharing conversations over a bite to eat, smelling the earth as my feet move across the ground through a pile of leaves, and just feeling the aliveness of everything around me. Why wish away all of this and rush to lay still, without any of my senses in the land of lonely stones?

It is our birthright to not only survive, but more to thrive and see the beauty of the world, even in its chaos. Keep in mind that there are ebbs and flows; that everything is in constant motion, things change as they should, and with patience, all misfortunes eventually lead to unalterable happiness. With that, I have discovered the presence of mind to fully breathe in the once never considered events of late. Enjoying my stepfather's company.

I tried to see my little nugget as much as possible. When mom felt confident enough, I was able to keep him for at least one weekend a month and if I got lucky, two weekends! During his visits, I made a point to take the baby to see Mario. For the first few months, the baby was terrified of him and did not want to leave my arms.

"He don't like me," Mario said with his loud and raspy voice.

"The loudness of your voice scares him."

"Oh really? Hmm."

After thinking about it, he agreed and toned it down. After more visits, I got the nugget, through playing little games, to interact with him. Now he was calling Mario "Papa" and I could tell that this meant the world to him. The baby was now sitting on his lap and giving him hugs as they shared babbling baby conversations. Mario looked at me and said, "If it weren't for you, this never would have happened." I smiled and said, "He needs to know his Papa!" Our eyes met and a strong sense of healing passed through both of us. We bonded. Both of us opened up and shared stories about our lives and discovered that we actually liked each other's company. We were in shock and awe that the two of us could even have such moments together. To finally forgive and fully understand one another seemed like a miracle. The animosity disappeared and the life-long burden was lifted. I felt exhilarated!

In the late summer of that year, Mario was diagnosed with liver cancer. I took him to doctor appointments, shopped for him, checked in on him, and when he went into the hospital, I paid his bills, cleaned his house and decorated for Christmas. He thought he had a few years but it was only weeks. Being there and watching him pass the way he did imprinted in my mind and that's all I could see. I'll spare the gory details, but I wondered why it worked out the way it did that I had to bear witness. Falling asleep was difficult and waking in the middle of the night was frequent. It took a while for me to come to terms. I thought about our veterans and troops and the horrors they carry in their heads. PTSD is real for sure! I knew that remembering and practicing all that I had learned before was imperative.

My backyard seemed the place to reconnect. It was 6am, laundry started, and the cats were fed. My coffee tasted exceptionally good that morning as the rising sun slowly colored the sky. Birds of all types sang and cooed in the stillness of the fresh, cool, damp air as the breeze gently woke the leaves on the trees.

There was a sense of peace within me which I hadn't felt so deeply since before my brother's transition. The feeling carried my thoughts to another time and place when I explored the wilderness on a hiking trail as my breath seemed to flow in and out of my heart rather than my nose.

"Thank you! I needed that!"

A sense of relief filled my body and the tension of the weeks prior faded, releasing any stiffness in my muscles. My head became free and clear of the stabbing pain between my eyes that had radiated and paralyzed my skull for months. *AHH! Nothing like being set free from a migraine!*

I basked in this wonderful moment in silence, stretching my neck and rolling my head from one side to the other. Slow, deep breaths filled my lungs as I reached for another sip of that glorious coffee.

"Geez. I should really cut the grass," as my eyes scanned the yard and landed on the ladder leaning on the fence, "and finish repainting the porch."

NO! I will not let my mind wander away from this beautiful moment and be hijacked into the world of "to do's" right now! Another bird song, another gentle stroke of the breeze over my skin.

"Meow. Meow. Meow," the cat called from the window sill. "Ding. Ding. Ding," the laundry is ready for the dryer.

It can wait. It can WAIT! One more sip of coffee. Shit! I have to pee! Really? I guess I need to get moving. "OK. You win for now."

It's always something right? What keeps me in check now is having a sense of humor about it. Having had so many deep cutting and difficult experiences throughout my life, I had no choice but to wave the white flag. When I lost my job in the midst of the Covid 19 crisis and the world was turned upside down with quarantine, sickness and death, what the hell else could I do? Yet, for some people, being forced to stay home gave lots of time for inner reflection. Many things came to the surface that promoted questions about who we have been, what we can or will choose to become, what we will tolerate and what we will not.

There will always be Yin and Yang; a positive vs negative and from the logical to the bizarre. As nature intends it to, this will never stop. Remembering this fact makes it easier to roll with the changes of life and have a good laugh along the way rather than falling into a negative perspective and getting stuck there. Throughout my life, I have realized that it is of no help for any of us to see ourselves only as victims, unlucky, continually being shit on, not good enough, misunderstood, etc.

Now that I have my little nephew, I worry less about myself and more for him. I think about all of the growing pains like being heartbroken for the first time, being deceived by a friend, peer pressure, experiencing the death of a cherished one, and on it goes. Of course, this is all necessary for him to feel and learn from. I want to protect him from all of it but know that this would be a huge disservice to his character and abilities to make wise future decisions. From this perspective, it is very clear to see and accept any hardships of my past.

One morning, I woke up staring at him in admiration. He was cuddled up close to my side, slowly returning to consciousness. It reminded me of myself when finally waking to start the day. He fussed and rubbed his eyes, squeezing them tight and tossing his head back and forth. His cute little whimpers and sounds expressed his displeasure for leaving that wonderful slumber. I thought, *I still do that EVERY morning!*

I lay next to him giggling to myself as I fully understood his irritation as he stirred. Then, as he opened his eyes and saw me, he immediately gave me a big smile as a sparkle widened his gaze. My heart sang, "Good morning and welcome to the day my little Nugget!"

More smiles. He inched his way over to my chest and cuddled up even tighter. I'd never felt better or more grateful. I looked up at the ceiling and thanked my brother for giving me this great gift. I saw his smile in my mind and felt that he would always be close. And he is!

Paying attention to synchronicities and vibes around me, as I had done in the past, makes my brother very visible to my spirit. He leaves me little trinkets and signs, more often when I'm having a bad day and can really use a pick-me-up. Most of the time, I get an overwhelming feeling to turn on the radio and right in that moment, the lyrics or content of the conversation are spot-on. Some people may think is weird or a bunch of crap. Others may think that it's all made up in my mind, but too many things have happened that leave no doubt in my mind that his spirit is alive and well. Throughout time, I have sensed the presence of my loved ones and find great comfort in the knowing that they are watching. Though my nephew hasn't met most of them, he points them out to me in a room or up in the sky. That's more than enough proof for me!

My little Nugget brings out the best in me and when I'm with him, all other distractions in my life become irrelevant. He is my teacher. I try to open my eyes and welcome the day and all it has to offer in wonder and joy, like he does. The inner child in me, that for so long had been injured, has now been reborn and given another chance to thrive. Seeing things through a happy child's eyes has certainly given me lots of laughs and a reminder to not be so intense when issues arise.

As yet another season of my life unfolds, I reflect on my blessings and give thanks for my journey. Losing my job of twenty years should have been devastating but as I continued on, I realized how life draining it really was. I'm in business for myself now and the future of my finances is a big question mark. Yet, a sort of calm has taken me over with a knowing that everything works out when I get out of my own way. I listen and follow my gut now, rather than following the mind that predicts how everything SHOULD happen. There are so many awesome surprises along the way when you just go with it. I fully appreciate this fact now and love being a participant

"I wish you peace when times are hard and a light to guide you through the dark." This is a song lyric by the Eagles from years ago that seems most appropriate to share with you as this book comes to a close.

May you be empowered to move through your journey with least resistance and live in happiness along the way. May you live, breathe and receive love always!

Namaste!

www.ingramcontent.com/pod-product-compliance
Lightning Source LLC
Chambersburg PA
CBHW021426070526
44577CB00001B/82